Metric units
and
conversion charts

Metric units
and
conversion charts

A metrication handbook
for engineers, technologists,
and scientists

second edition

Theodore Wildi

President, Sperika Enterprises Ltd.

Professor Emeritus of Laval University
Department of Electrical Engineering

IEEE
PRESS

The Institute of Electrical and Electronics Engineers, Inc. New York

IEEE PRESS
445 Hoes Lane, P. O. Box 1331
Piscataway, New Jersey 08855-1331

© 1995, 1991, 1988 by Sperika Enterprises Ltd.
© 1973, 1972, 1971 by Volta, Inc.

Printed in the United States of America

10 9 8 7 6 5 4 3 2

ISBN 0-7803-1050-0

IEEE Order Number: PP4044

Library of Congress Cataloging-in-Publication Data
Wildi, Theodore
  Metric units and conversion charts : a metrication handbook for
engineers, technologists, and scientists / Theodore Wildi. --2nd
ed.
    p.   cm.
   Includes bibliographical references and index.
   ISBN 0-7803-1050-0
   1. Metric system--Conversion tables--Handbooks, manuals, etc.
I. Title
QC94.W53   1995
530.8' 12--dc20   95-3182
                                             CIP

To my son Karl,

*for his invaluable help in
the creation of my books*

PREFACE

Everything we produce and consume, everything we buy and sell, and everything we see and feel is measured and compared by means of units. Units enable us to measure the distance we walk, the land we own, the time of day and the brightness of stars – and in fact every feature of our activities and of the environment in which we live.

The various measurement systems developed throughout the world have produced a large number of units. This handbook shows in an exceptionally clear and useful way how these units are related to each other, and how they are defined. One of its principal advantages lies in the conversion of units, a process made exceedingly simple by a set of conversion charts. They enable the engineer, scientist and technician to make rapid and clear-cut conversions between units of the American Customary system, the English system, former metric systems, and the International System of Units (SI).

The conversion charts rank the units by order of size so that the relationship between any two units can be found quickly and without ambiguity. They significantly reduce the time usually needed to consult handbooks, tables and other reference books, in solving engineering and scientific problems.

The information contained herein is based upon the latest data on units and quantities published by the American National Standards Institute (ANSI), The Institute of Electrical and Electronics Engineers (IEEE), the Bureau international des poids et mesures (BIPM), the Committee on Data for Science and Technology (CODATA) and by ISO, the International Organization for Standardization.

This second edition of *Metric Units and Conversion Charts* contains important additions and changes. They are listed as follows:

1) quantity equations and numerical equations are explained in separate chapters, and in much greater detail, together with worked-out examples

2) the recommended symbols for quantities are shown at the top of each chart

3) the charts identify the non-SI units that may be used along with the SI

4) the fundamental conversion process is explained in Chapter 3

5) a section explains thermodynamic, Celsius, and Fahrenheit temperatures, and how their numerical and quantity equations are applied

6) a separate chapter has been added to show how derived units are expressed in terms of base units

7) a new chapter on Mass, Force and Gravity explains how the units of force were determined

8) more than 100 review questions are provided, together with answers.

The conversion charts, devised by me in 1970, have been used by many engineers, scientists and students. In this regard, most people consider the adoption of the International System of Units (SI) to be merely a question of learning some rules and converting pounds into kilograms and inches into centimeters. This is a relatively simple exercise that only requires the relevant conversion factor to be correctly applied.

However, conversions are related to the equally important process of working with quantity equations and numerical equations in which the latter comprise a plethora of units.

Consider, for example, the following equation, taken from a handbook, that gives the velocity V of air (in feet per second), at an atmospheric pressure P_b (in inches of mercury) in an ambient temperature T (in degrees Rankine), under a velocity pressure P_v (in inches of water):

$$V = 15.9 \sqrt{\frac{P_v T}{P_b}}$$

Suppose we wish to express this equation in SI units, with $V_{(SI)}$ in meters per second, $P_{v(SI)}$ and $P_{b(SI)}$ in pascals, and $T_{(SI)}$ in kelvins. This is best done by following the procedure described in Chapter 5. The answer is:

$$V_{(SI)} = 23.9 \sqrt{\frac{P_{v(SI)} T_{(SI)}}{P_{b(SI)}}}$$

Making such a transformation is not difficult, but neither is it trivial. In effect, unless a structured methodology is employed, considerable time may be required to solve such a problem, to ensure the answer is correct.

Thus, in the technical, engineering, and scientific world, the question of converting to SI units goes far beyond the simple conversion of calories into joules. Because of this, I believe that the process of conversion (and the distinction between quantity equations and numerical equations) should be taught in every physics course, or in one of the early freshman programs.

Some community colleges and universities are already devoting a few hours to cover this important topic. It is hoped that other institutions will examine their learning programs with a view to including the study of quantity equations and numerical equations in one of their courses. A two- or three-hour session devoted to this subject will be of lasting benefit to the future engineer, scientist, or technician.

I believe that such a plan of action is also an effective way of introducing and promoting the SI. Furthermore, it provides the tools needed to utilize the vast technical literature that preceded the inception of the SI system of units. In effect, the advent of SI does not enable us to scrap the handbooks and textbooks and papers and patents that were written before this new system was introduced. Nor can we change, overnight, the thinking processes of a generation that has been accustomed to the American Customary system of measure. We are obliged, therefore, to work with a hybrid variety of units for some years to come, and it is the purpose of this book to make the task a little easier.

*   *   *

I want to express my gratitude to the many individuals who offered their helpful comments. In particular, I want to thank Mr. K.C. Ford, Professor Mario Iona, Mr. Guy-W. Richard, Dr. Bruce B. Barrow, Dr. Chester H. Page, Professor Groves E. Herrick, and Dr. Gilles Y. Delisle for their important contributions.

The approach used in this book is properly that of the author, and may at times diverge from individual assessments or opinions. However, from a technical standpoint, the book is believed to be essentially free of error.

I am also happy to acknowledge the support of the staff of IEEE Press, and in particular that of Mr. Dudley R. Kay, Director of Book Publishing.

Last but not least, I want to thank my wife for her moral support, and my son Karl for putting the manuscript and charts into computerized form.

Theodore Wildi

CONTENTS

1

INTRODUCING THE
CONVERSION CHARTS

1.1 Quantities and Units

In order to make metric conversions, it is useful to know what is meant by quantities and units.

A *physical quantity* is any physical property that can be measured. Length, time, force and temperature are examples of the some 400 physical quantities that describe our physical world. The magnitude of a quantity may be large or small. For example, a quantity such as the mass of a truck is greater than the mass of a fly.

A *unit* is a quantity that has a specific, defined magnitude. Thus, the meter is a quantity of length whose magnitude is defined in the following way:

> The meter (m) is the length of the path travelled by light in vacuum during a time interval of 1/299 792 458 of a second.

Because the meter has a specific magnitude, it can be used as a measuring stick to describe the length of anything. However, the meter is not the only unit used to measure length. As civilizations evolved, various units of length were devised. Their magnitudes were such as to make them convenient measuring sticks for whatever had to be measured. Thus, units of length such as the inch, the mile, the ångström were created to respectively measure small, large and infinitesimal lengths.

The many units of length are displayed in the chart on page 25. Each unit is represented by a box, and the boxes are arranged so that the largest unit is at the top, the smallest at the bottom and intermediate units are ranked in between.

The units are connected by arrows, each of which bears a number. This number is the ratio of the larger to the smaller of the units that are connected, and so its value is always greater than one. The arrow always points toward the smaller of the two units which it connects.

The ordered display of these units of length, showing their relative magnitudes, is called a *conversion chart*. Similar conversion charts for mass, force, pressure and some 60 other quantities are featured in this book. The charts appear in alphabetical order. Using these conversion charts, it is very easy to convert a quantity expressed in one particular unit into any other unit. Naturally, the conversion must involve units of the same kind – inches into meters, or kilograms into ounces and not, say, ounces into meters. We now explain how the conversion charts are used.

1.2 Methodology

Figure 1 shows a simple conversion chart involving only six units of length - the mile, meter, yard, foot, inch and millimeter*. The units, represented by boxes, are positioned in descending order of size. The numbers beside the arrows show the relative magnitude of the connected units; the yard is 3 times larger than the foot, the foot is 12 times larger than the inch, and so on. With this arrangement we can convert a quantity expressed in terms of a UNIT A into the same quantity expressed in terms of another UNIT B, by the following simple procedure.

Starting from UNIT A we follow the arrows along *any path* that ends up at UNIT B. In so doing, we sometimes move with, and sometimes against, the direction of the arrows. When moving in the direction of an arrow we *multiply* the number associated with it; when moving against the arrow we *divide*. In other words, we observe the simple rule:

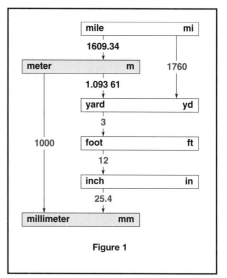

    with the arrow   MULTIPLY
against the arrow   DIVIDE

Because the arrows in Figure 1 point downwards, we multiply when moving down the chart, and divide when moving up.

Figure 1

Example 1-1:

Convert a quantity of 2.5 feet into millimeters.

Solution:

Starting from **foot** and moving towards **millimeter** we obviously move in the same direction as the arrows numbered 12 and 25.4. We must therefore *multiply* the numbers associated with each arrow:

$$2.5 \text{ feet} = 2.5 \,(\times \; 12)\,(\times \; 25.4) \text{ millimeters}$$
$$= 762 \text{ millimeters}$$

Example 1-2:

Convert 95 040 inches into miles.

Solution:

Starting from **inch** and moving toward **mile**, we can follow a path involving the

---

* In most English-speaking countries, including Canada, the SI unit of length is spelled metre, and a unit of volume is spelled litre. On the other hand, the spelling of these two units in the United States is often meter and liter. In this book, we have adopted the meter, liter spelling.

arrows 12, 3 and 1760. Since we are moving against the direction of the arrows, we *divide* by the number associated with each arrow:

$$95\ 040 \text{ inches} = 95\ 040\ (\div\ 12)\ (\div\ 3)\ (\div\ 1760) \text{ miles}$$

$$= \frac{95\ 040}{12\ \times\ 3\ \times\ 1760} \text{ miles}$$

$$= 1.5 \text{ miles}$$

1.3 Flyers

When we have to convert units that are far apart on a conversion chart, several multiplications or divisions must be made. To reduce the arithmetic, "flyers" are introduced to bypass a series of units. A flyer is simply another arrow that bears a number, whose value is equal to the product of the numbers which the flyer bypasses. In Figure 1, for example, the flyer 1000 joining **meter** and **millimeter** is equal to the product of the numbers $1.093\ 61 \times 3 \times 12 \times 25.4$.

Flyers provide additional paths between units, and any of these paths may be followed without affecting the conversion result.

Example 1-3:

Convert a quantity of 750 inches into meters.

Solution (a):

In moving from **inch** to **meter**, we can follow the path involving arrows 12, 3 and 1.093 61. Because we move against each arrow, we must divide, as follows:

$$750 \text{ inches} = 750\ (\div\ 12)\ (\div\ 3)\ (\div\ 1.093\ 61)$$
$$= 19.05 \text{ meters}$$

Solution (b):

We can also move from **inch** to **meter** by taking a path that involves arrows 25.4 and 1000. In so doing, we move along arrow 25.4 (hence multiply) but we move against arrow 1000 (hence divide). The conversion result is:

$$750 \text{ inches} = 750\ (\times\ 25.4)\ (\div\ 1000)$$
$$= 19.05 \text{ meters}$$

Note that solution (b) using the flyer is quicker then solution (a) because it involves only one multiplication and one division rather than three divisions.

1.4 SI units

SI units and their multiples and submultiples appear in *red* boxes in the conversion charts. Because they are connected by flyers that are multiples of ten, it is possible to move swiftly from one end of a chart to the other should a conversion between widely separated units be required. American customary units and non-SI metric units can be converted to SI or vice versa by the technique we have just described.

1.5 Symbols of quantities

The symbols of quantities are shown along with the name of the quantity at the top of each conversion chart. For example, the symbols for Length (page 25) are l, b, d, h, r, s, and w. By convention, the letter symbols of quantities are in italics.

1.6 Symbols of units

The symbols for all SI units (and for many non-SI units) appear on the right-hand side of each box. Symbols have been omitted whenever a clear and authoritative consensus was lacking. By convention, the symbols of units are in roman (upright) typeface.

1.7 Numerical values

Numerical values of the arrows are shown either in red or in black.

  RED numbers are exact, by definition.

  BLACK numbers are accurate to the number of significant figures shown.

A useful feature of the charts is that exact conversion accuracy between units can be obtained by following paths that involve red numbers. These paths are usually erratic, and may require one or more multiplications and divisions.

For example, referring to the chart on LENGTH, page 25, we find that

1 meter = 1 ($\times$ 1.093 61) ($\times$ 3) ($\times$ 12) = 39.3699 inches (6-figure accuracy). But if we follow a path involving red numbers we find that

1 meter = 1 ($\times$ 100) ($\div$ 2.54) = 39.370 078 $\cdots$ inches *exactly*.

1.8 Writing numbers

To simplify the reading of numbers having many digits, the digits are set in groups of three, separated by a space. The spaces are counted to the left and to the right of the decimal marker. A space is not necessary when only four digits precede or follow the decimal marker. If a number is less than one, a zero must precede the decimal marker.

This style eliminates the need for commas as group separators. For example, we write

13 754 instead of 13754 or 13,754

25 146.241 32 instead of 25146.24132 or 25,146.24132

From an international standpoint, this *group-of-three* rule also prevents confusion because many countries use the comma as a decimal marker.

1.9 Converting to SI base units

The SI unit of any quantity can be expressed in terms of one or more of the seven SI base units. This expression in terms of SI base units is shown in brackets on the left-hand side of the box that displays the SI unit. For example, referring to the chart on ENERGY, page 19, we see that the expression for the joule in terms of SI base units is [kg·m^2/s^2] *. This relationship is more than one of simple

---

* It is customary to show the product of two units by a raised dot. When this is not possible, a simple dot on the line is acceptable.

equivalence: one joule is *exactly* equal to 1 kg·m^2/s^2. Similarly, the SI unit of force, the newton (page 24), can be expressed as N = kg·m/s^2.

Example 1-4:

Express a heat loss of 1750 Btu per hour in terms of the appropriate SI unit. Show its symbol and express the result in terms of SI base units (see page 34) .

Solution:

The SI unit corresponding to the Btu is the watt and its symbol W is shown in the box. The expression in terms of SI base units is [kg·m^2/s^3]. We therefore have:

$$1750 \text{ Btu per hour} = 1750 \ (\div 3.414\ 43) \text{ W}$$

$$= 512.53 \text{ W} = 512.53 \text{ kg} \cdot \text{m}^2/\text{s}^3$$

Example 1-5:

Convert an area of 3 square miles into hectares (see page 12). Give the value, correct to 9 significant figures, and show the appropriate unit symbols.

Solution:

Since we want an answer correct to 9 significant figures, we must follow a path involving only red numbers. The units are mi^2 and ha. We therefore obtain:

$$3 \text{ mi}^2 = 3(\times 16)(\times 40)(\times 43\ 560)(\times 144)(\times 6.4516)(\div 10^4)(\div 10^6)(\times 100) \text{ ha}$$

$$= \frac{1920 \times 43\ 560 \times 144 \times 6.4516 \times 100}{10^{10}} \text{ ha}$$

$$= 776.996\ 433 \text{ ha}$$

1.10   Classification of SI units, and other names for the SI units and their multiples and submultiples

It is important to emphasize that each physical quantity has only one SI unit. However, this unit (and its multiples and submultiples) can often be expressed in more than one form. For example, the SI unit of pressure is the *pascal*, but it can also be expressed in the form *newton per square meter*, which involves two SI units. In order to distinguish between the SI unit proper (and its multiples and submultiples) and other SI forms in which they may be expressed, we have created two types of boxes, as follows:

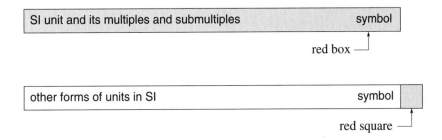

1.11 Classification of non-SI units

In textbooks and other publications, it is recommended that only SI units be employed. However, some units such as minute, hour, day, liter, tonne, and the angular measures degree, minute and second, can be used along with the SI.

Other non-SI units may be used along with SI for a certain time*. They are: nautical mile, knot, ångström, barn, bar, gal, curie, roentgen, rad, rem, are and hectare. This distinction is here made by identifying the boxes in the following way:

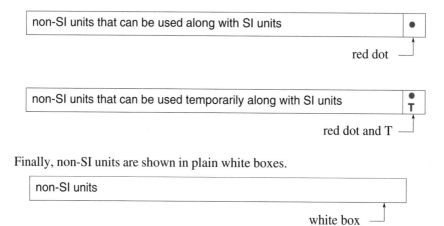

| non-SI units that can be used along with SI units | ● |

red dot ⌐

| non-SI units that can be used temporarily along with SI units | ●
T |

red dot and T ⌐

Finally, non-SI units are shown in plain white boxes.

| non-SI units |

white box ⌐

REVIEW QUESTIONS

1.1   Convert a pressure of 30 lbf/in^2 into atmospheres (use chart, page 34).

1.2   An electric heater is rated at 1500 watts. Express this in Btu per hour.

1.3   Express 1 ton of refrigeration in Btu per minute (use chart, page 34).

1.4   A flywheel has a moment of inertia of 120 gf·cm·s^2. Express it in lb·ft^2.

1.5   Convert 500 troy ounces into kilograms to give 8-figure accuracy.

1.6   Give the quantity symbols for mass, electric field strength, and power.

1.7   Give the SI symbols for the units of mass, electric field strength, and power.

1.8   Express the pascal, the centipoise, and the knot in terms of SI base units.

1.9   a) Express a temperature of 72°F in degrees Celsius (use chart, page 40).
        b) Express a temperature rise of 72°F in degrees Celsius.

1.10 Express 40 fluid ounces (U.S.) in liters (use chart, page 46).

Rewrite the following numbers according to the group-of-three space rule:

1.11   17.00362

1.12   17463

1.13   987654321.12345678

1.14   1700.36429

---

* Some standards-setting bodies elect to modify the status of the units that the CIPM (Comité international des poids et mesures) permits to be used temporarily with the SI.

Conversion Charts

SI unit, and its multiples and submultiples:	RED BOX	
other forms of units in SI:	RED SQUARE	
units that may be used along with the SI:	RED DOT	•
units that may be used temporarily along with the SI:	RED DOT + T	• T
non – SI units:	ALL – WHITE BOX	

RED NUMBERS are exact, by definition

BLACK NUMBERS are accurate to the number of significant figures shown

Conversion Rule

WITH THE ARROW – MULTIPLY

AGAINST THE ARROW – DIVIDE

SI PREFIXES
SYMBOLS AND VALUES

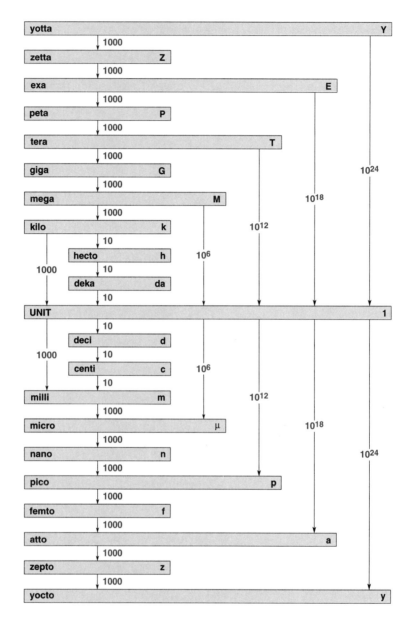

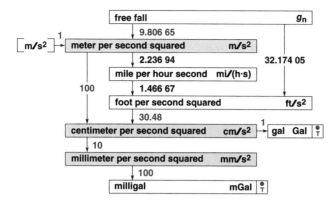

AMOUNT OF SUBSTANCE (n)

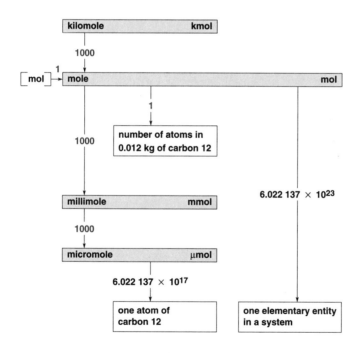

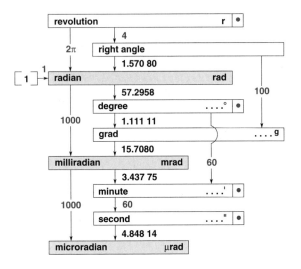

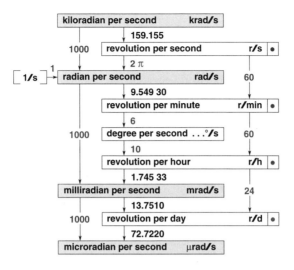

Example: convert 1800 revolutions per minute to radians per second
Solution: 1800 r/min = 1800 (÷ 9.549 30) rad/s = 188.495 rad/s

ANGULAR FREQUENCY (ω)
CIRCULAR FREQUENCY
PULSATANCE

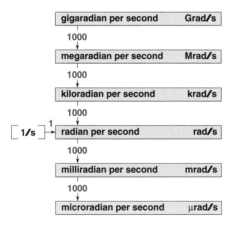

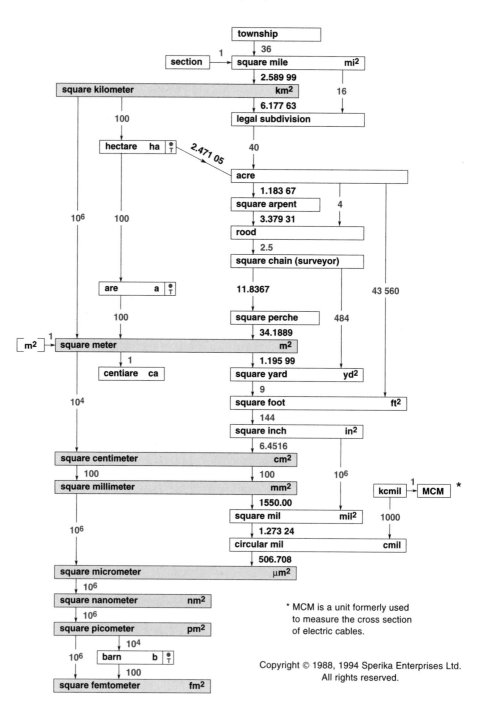

| township |
| 1 → 36 ↓ |

section → **square mile** mi²

2.589 99

square kilometer km² → 16

6.177 63

legal subdivision

100 → hectare ha 2.471 05 40

acre

1.183 67

square arpent 4

10⁶ 100 3.379 31

rood

2.5

square chain (surveyor) 43 560

are a 11.8367

100 **square perche** 484

34.1889

1 **square meter** m²

1 1.195 99

centiare ca **square yard** yd²

10⁴ 9

square foot ft²

144

square inch in²

6.4516

square centimeter cm²

100 100 10⁶

square millimeter mm² kcmil →¹ **MCM** *

1550.00

square mil mil² 1000

10⁶ 1.273 24

circular mil cmil

506.708

square micrometer μm²

10⁶

square nanometer nm²

10⁶

square picometer pm²

10⁴

10⁶ **barn** b

100

square femtometer fm²

* MCM is a unit formerly used
to measure the cross section
of electric cables.

Example: Convert 4 square miles to hectares
Solution: 4 mi² = 4 (× 2.589 99) (× 100) ha = 1036 hectares

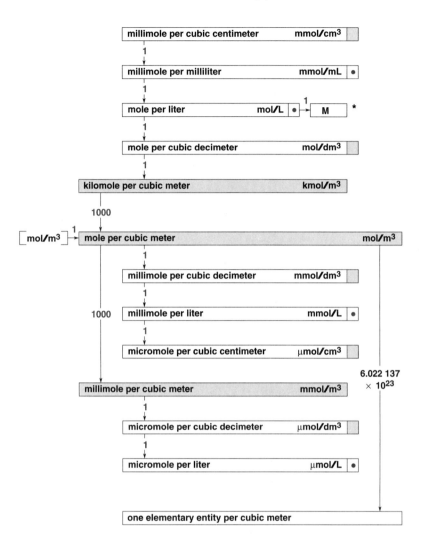

* The term molarity was formerly used to express concentration in moles of solute per liter of solution.

DENSITY (mass per unit volume) (ρ)

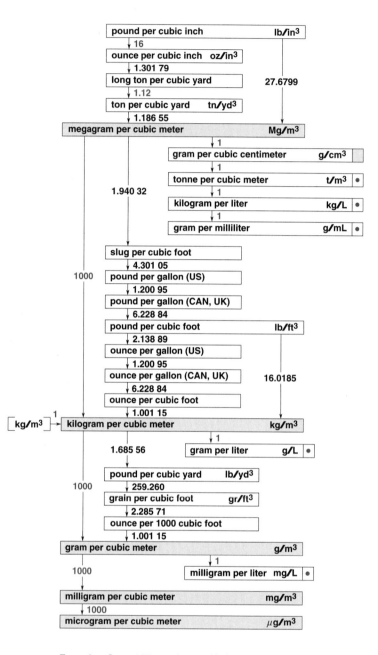

Example: Convert 60 pounds per cubic foot to tons per cubic yard

Solution: 60 lb/ft³ = 60 ($\times$ 16.0185) ($\div$ 1000) ($\div$ 1.186 55) = 0.81 tn/yd³

RESISTANCE (*R*)

CONDUCTANCE (*G*)

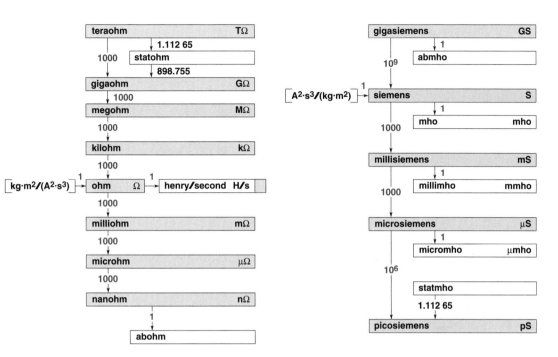

INDUCTANCE (*L*)

CAPACITANCE (*C*)

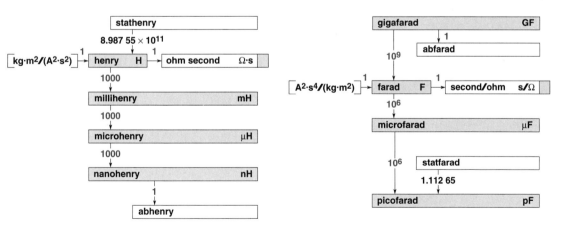

ELECTRICITY

CURRENT DENSITY (J)

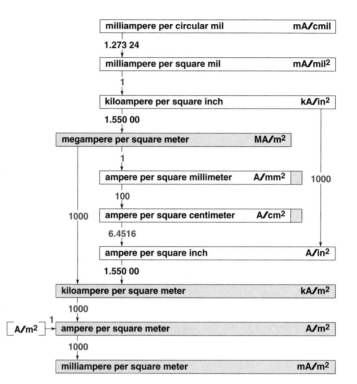

milliampere per circular mil	mA/cmil

1.273 24

milliampere per square mil	mA/mil²

1

kiloampere per square inch	kA/in²

1.550 00

megampere per square meter	MA/m²

1

ampere per square millimeter	A/mm²	1000

100

ampere per square centimeter	A/cm²

6.4516

ampere per square inch	A/in²

1.550 00

kiloampere per square meter	kA/m²

1000

$\boxed{\text{A/m}^2}$ → 1 → | ampere per square meter | A/m² |

1000

milliampere per square meter	mA/m²

ELECTRIC FIELD STRENGTH (E)

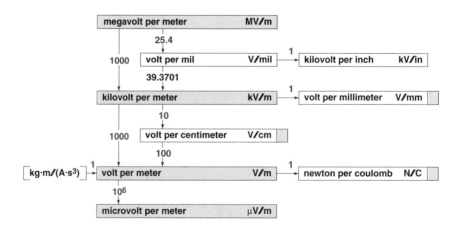

megavolt per meter	MV/m

25.4

1000 → | volt per mil | V/mil | → 1 → | kilovolt per inch | kV/in |

39.3701

kilovolt per meter	kV/m	→ 1 →	volt per millimeter	V/mm

10

1000 → | volt per centimeter | V/cm |

100

$\boxed{\text{kg·m/(A·s}^3)}$ → 1 → | volt per meter | V/m | → 1 → | newton per coulomb | N/C |

10⁶

microvolt per meter	µV/m

ELECTRICITY

CURRENT (I)

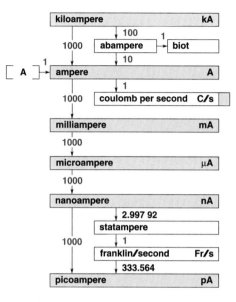

CHARGE (Q)

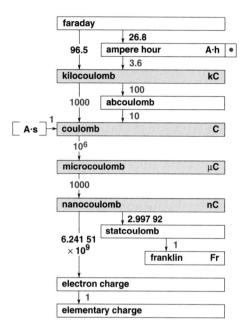

ELECTROMOTIVE FORCE (E)

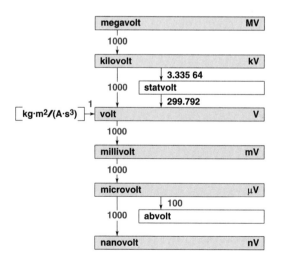

Example: Express 3 kilovolts in terms of SI base units

Solution: 3 kV = 3 (× 1000) (× 1) kg·m²/(A·s³) = 3000 kg·m²/(A·s³)

RESISTIVITY (ρ)

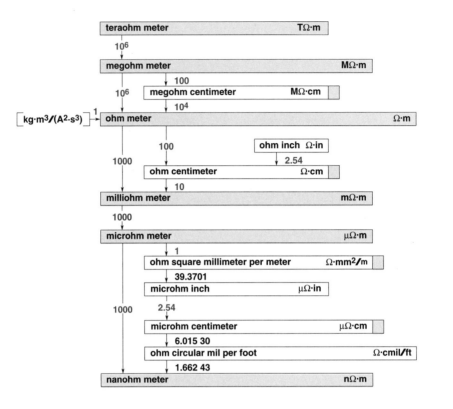

Example: Convert 60 ohm circular mil per foot to ohm centimeter

Solution: 60 Ωcmil/ft = 60 ($\times$ 1.662 43) ($\div$ 1000) ($\div$ 1000) ($\div$ 10) = 9.974 58 $\times$ 10^{-6} Ω·cm

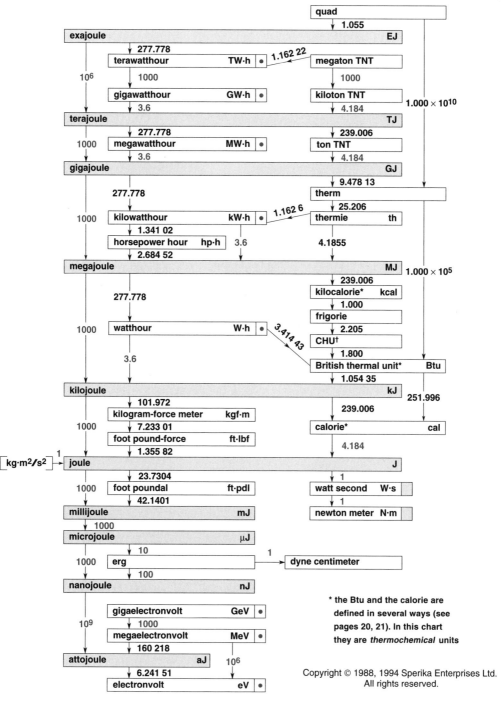

* the Btu and the calorie are defined in several ways (see pages 20, 21). In this chart they are *thermochemical* units

† CHU (°C Heat Unit) is the heat required to raise the temperature of 1 lb of water 1°C

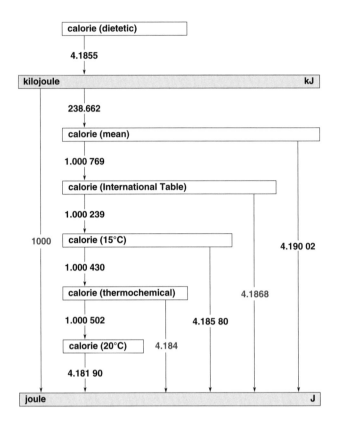

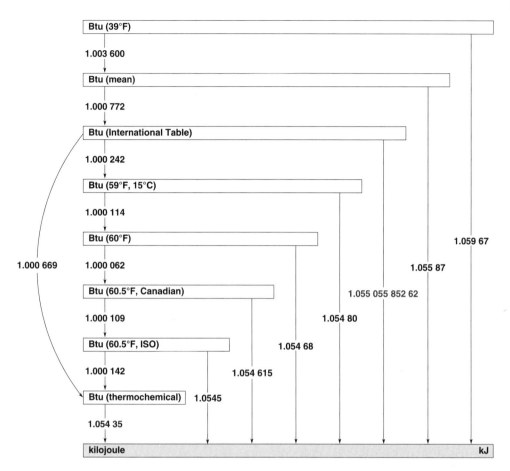

Example: Convert 4000 Btu (60°F) to Btu (thermochemical)

Solution: 4000 Btu (60°F) = 4000 (× 1.054 68) (÷ 1.054 35) Btu (thermochemical) = 4001.25 Btu (thermochemical)

c = speed of light in vacuum = $2.997\ 924\ 58 \times 10^8$ m/s = {c} m/s

k = Boltzmann constant = $1.380\ 658 \times 10^{-23}$ J/K = {k} J/K

h = Planck constant = $6.626\ 0755 \times 10^{-34}$ J·s = {h} J·s

c_2 = second radiation constant = $1.438\ 769 \times 10^{-2}$ m·K = {c_2} m·K

N_A = Avogadro constant = $6.022\ 1367 \times 10^{23}$ mol^{-1} = {N_A} mol^{-1}

R_∞ = Rydberg constant = $1.097\ 3731 \times 10^7$ m^{-1} = {R_∞} m^{-1}

{ } = numerical value of constant when the constant is expressed in SI units

cal_{th} = thermochemical calorie (see page 19)

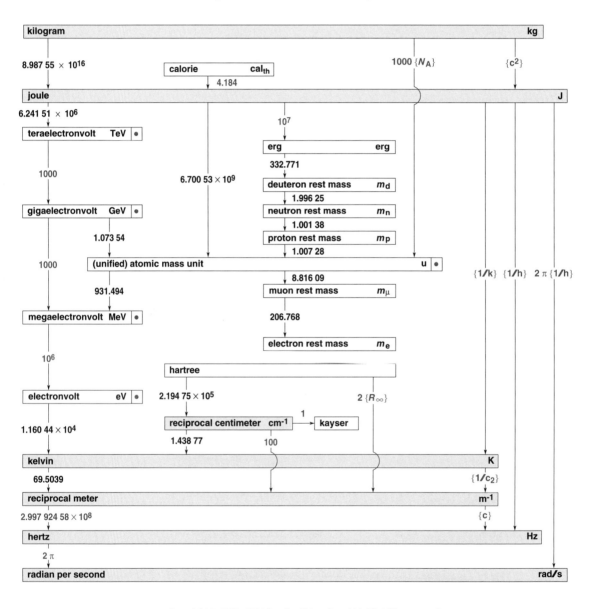

FLOW RATE (q_v)

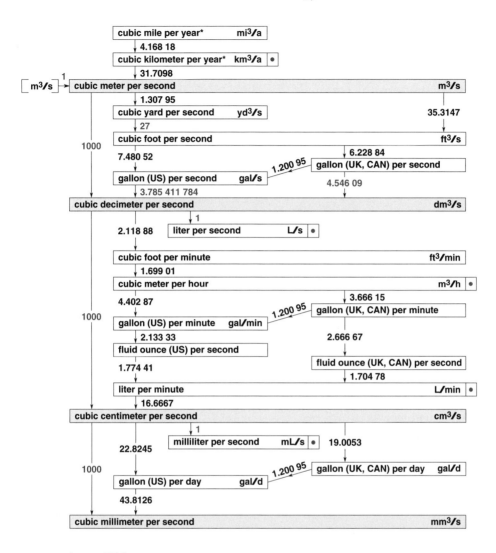

*year = 365 days

Note: UK, CAN stands for United Kingdom, Canada

Example: Convert 250 gallons (US) per minute to liters per second
Solution: 250 gal (US)/min = 250 (× 2.133 33) (× 1.774 41) (× 16.6667) (÷ 1000) (× 1) L/s = 15.7725 L/s

FORCE (*F*)

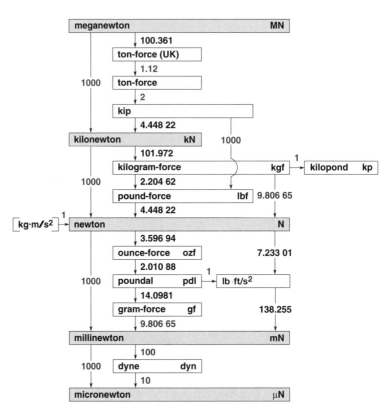

Example: Convert 30 pound-force to newtons
Solution: 30 pound-force = 30 (× 4.448 22) N = 133.447 N

FREQUENCY (*f*)

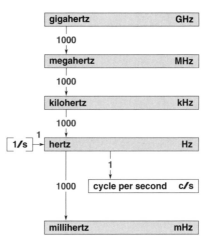

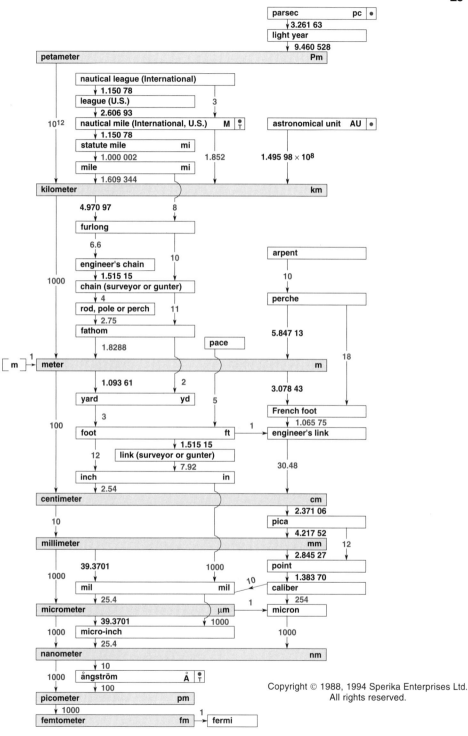

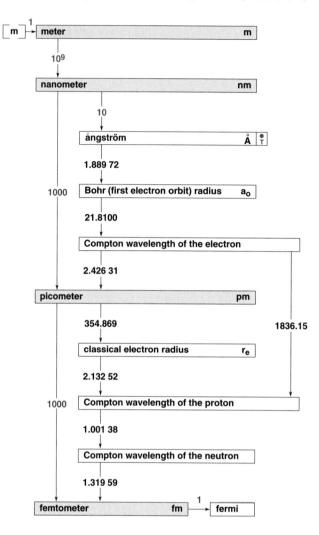

Example: Express the Bohr first electron radius (a_o) in fermis

Solution: $a_o = 1 \, (\times \, 21.8100) \, (\times \, 2.426 \, 31) \, (\times \, 1000) \, (\times \, 1)$ fermi $= 52 \, 917.8$ fermi

LIGHT

LUMINANCE (L, L_v)

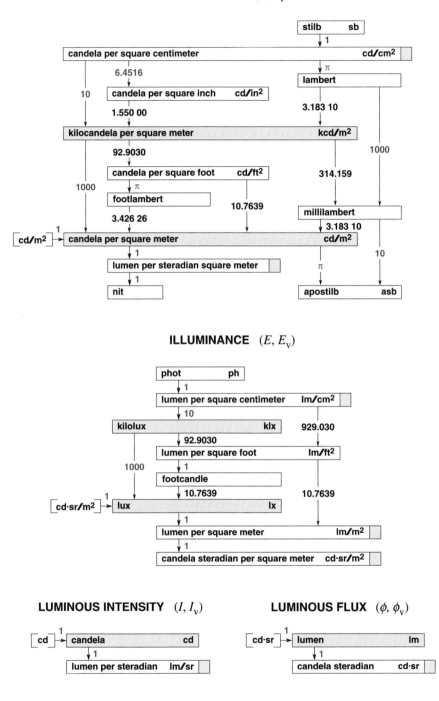

ILLUMINANCE (E, E_v)

LUMINOUS INTENSITY (I, I_v)

LUMINOUS FLUX (ϕ, ϕ_v)

MAGNETIC MOMENT (atomic units and quantities) (μ)

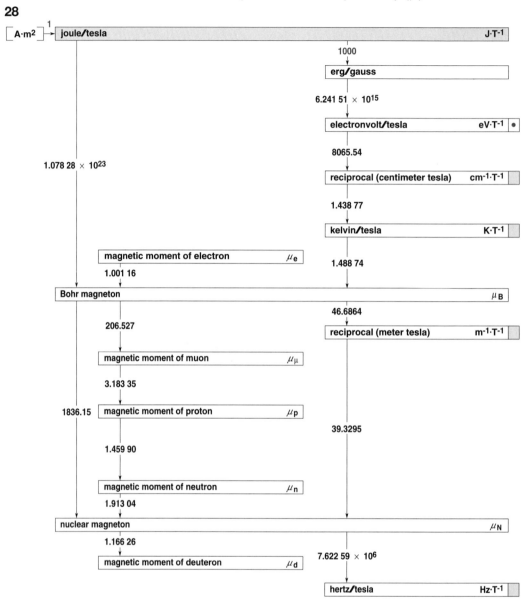

MAGNETISM

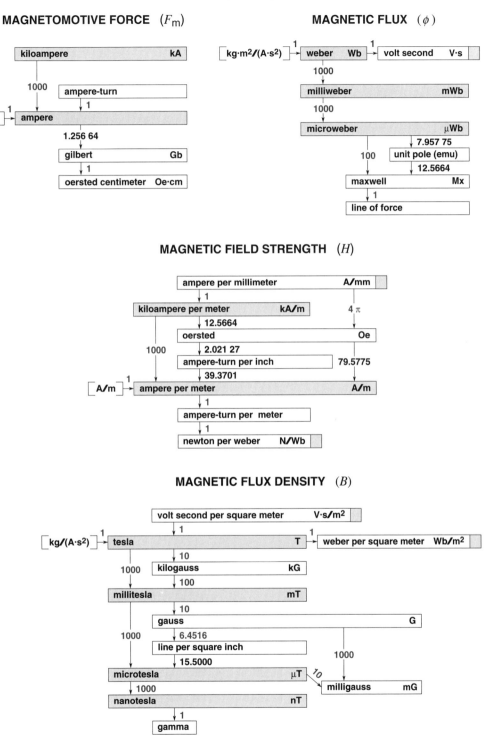

MAGNETOMOTIVE FORCE (F_m)

kiloampere	kA

1000

ampere-turn	

1

A → ampere (1)

1.256 64

gilbert	Gb

1

oersted centimeter	Oe·cm

MAGNETIC FLUX (ϕ)

$[kg \cdot m^2/(A \cdot s^2)]$ →(1)→ weber Wb →(1)→ volt second V·s

1000

milliweber	mWb

1000

microweber	μWb

7.957 75

unit pole (emu)	

100   12.5664

maxwell	Mx

1

line of force	

MAGNETIC FIELD STRENGTH (H)

ampere per millimeter	A/mm

1

kiloampere per meter	kA/m

12.5664   4 π

oersted	Oe

1000   2.021 27

ampere-turn per inch	79.5775

39.3701

A/m →(1)→ ampere per meter | A/m |

1

ampere-turn per meter	

1

newton per weber	N/Wb

MAGNETIC FLUX DENSITY (B)

volt second per square meter	V·s/m²

1

$[kg/(A \cdot s^2)]$ →(1)→ tesla T →(1)→ weber per square meter Wb/m²

10

1000 | kilogauss | kG |

100

millitesla	mT

10

gauss	G

1000   6.4516

line per square inch	

15.5000   1000

microtesla	μT

10 → | milligauss | mG |

1000

nanotesla	nT

1

gamma	

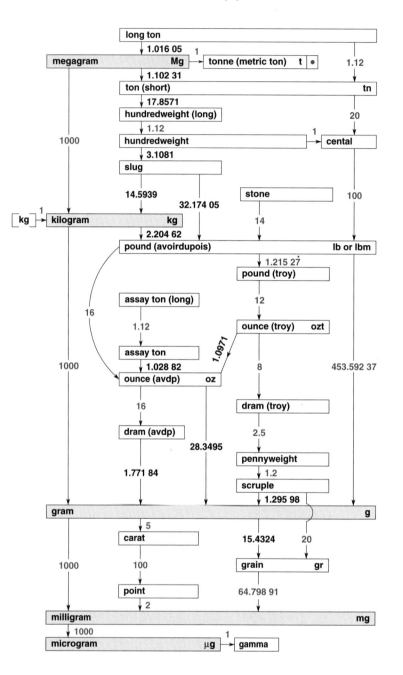

Example: Convert 2 kilograms to troy ounces **exactly**

Solution: For exact conversions we follow the arrows bearing red numbers. Thus:

2 kg = 2 (× 1000) (× 1000) (÷ 64.798 91) (÷ 20) (÷ 1.2) (÷ 2.5) (÷ 8) ozt = 64.301 49 . . . . ozt

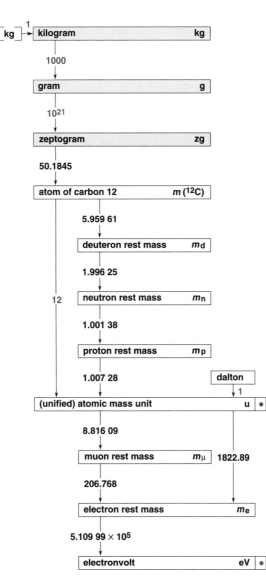

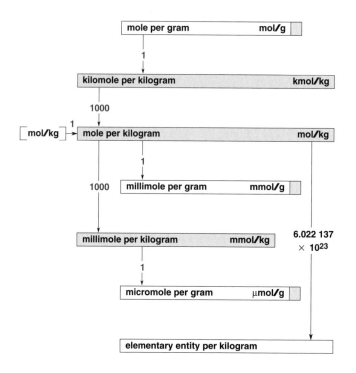

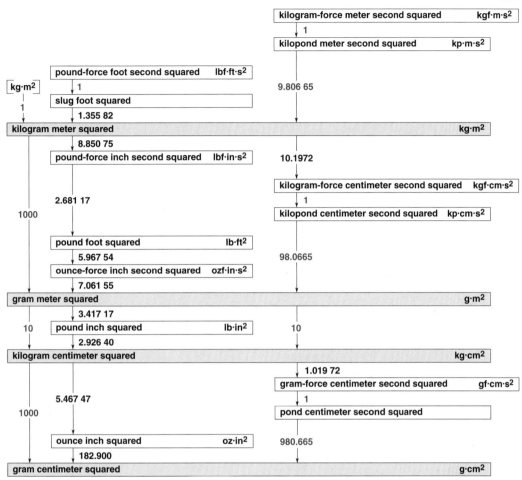

Example: Convert 80 pound-foot squared into kilogram meter squared

Solution: 80 lb·ft² = 80 (× 5.967 54) (× 7.061 55) (÷ 1000) kg·m² = 3.371 21 kg·m²

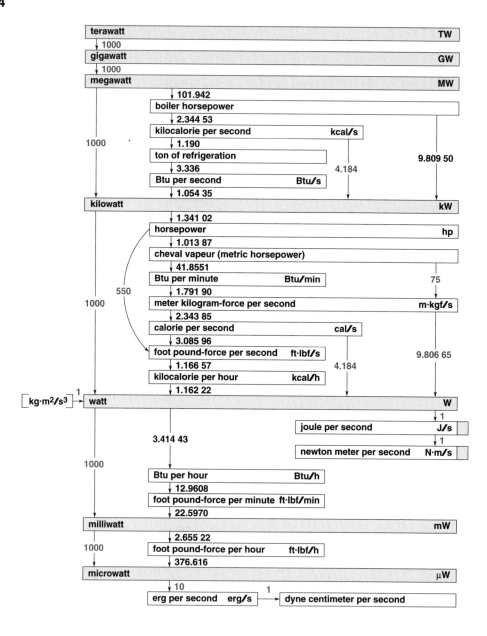

Note: the Btu and the calorie are defined in several ways (see pages 20, 21). In this chart they are *thermochemical* units

Example: Convert 12 boiler horsepower into kilowatts

Solution: 12 boiler hp = 12 (÷ 101.942) (× 1000) kW = 117.714 kW

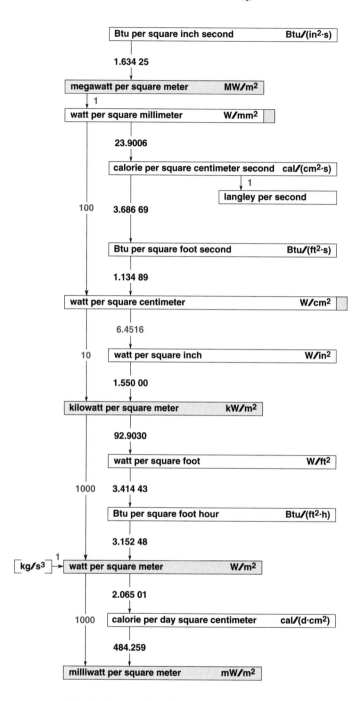

Btu per square inch second   Btu/(in²·s)

1.634 25

megawatt per square meter   MW/m²

1

watt per square millimeter   W/mm²

23.9006

calorie per square centimeter second   cal/(cm²·s)

1

langley per second

100   3.686 69

Btu per square foot second   Btu/(ft²·s)

1.134 89

watt per square centimeter   W/cm²

6.4516

10   watt per square inch   W/in²

1.550 00

kilowatt per square meter   kW/m²

92.9030

watt per square foot   W/ft²

1000   3.414 43

Btu per square foot hour   Btu/(ft²·h)

3.152 48

kg/s³ → 1   watt per square meter   W/m²

2.065 01

1000   calorie per day square centimeter   cal/(d·cm²)

484.259

milliwatt per square meter   mW/m²

Note: the Btu and the calorie are defined in several ways (see
pages 20, 21). In this chart they are *thermochemical* units

POWER (horsepower units) (P)

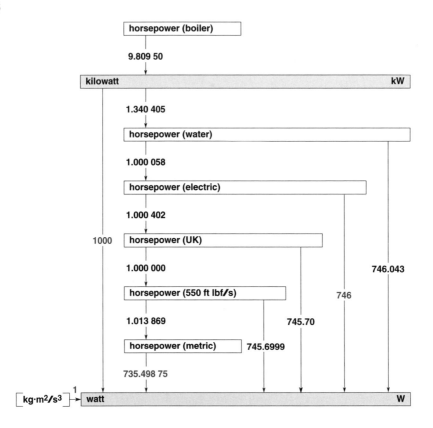

POWER LEVEL DIFFERENCE or FIELD LEVEL DIFFERENCE (D)

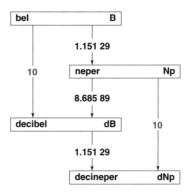

Example 1: Convert 80 decibels to nepers
Solution : 80 dB = 80 (÷ 8.685 89) Np = 9.21 Np

Example 2: Convert 7 nepers to decibels
Solution : 7 Np = 7 (× 8.685 89) dB = 60.80 dB

PRESSURE AND STRESS (p)

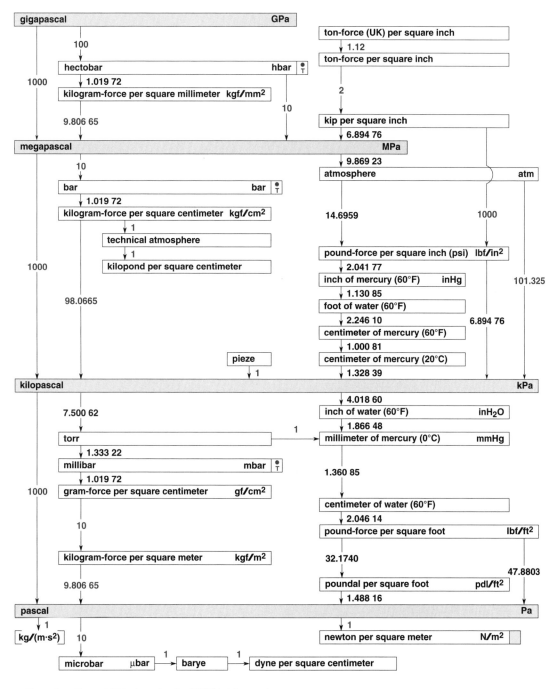

Example: Convert 15 inches of water (60°F) to kilopascals

Solution: 15 inH₂O (60°F) = 15 (÷ 4.018 60) = 3.732 64 kPa

DOSE EQUIVALENT (H)

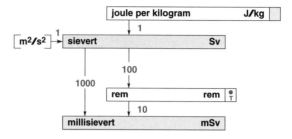

ACTIVITY (of radionuclides) (A)

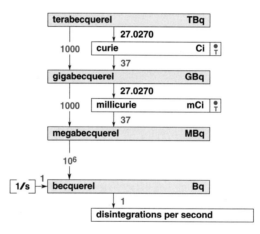

Example: Convert 5 millicuries to gigabecquerels

Solution: 5 mCi = 5 (÷ 27.0270) GBq = 0.185 GBq

RADIOLOGY

EXPOSURE (X)

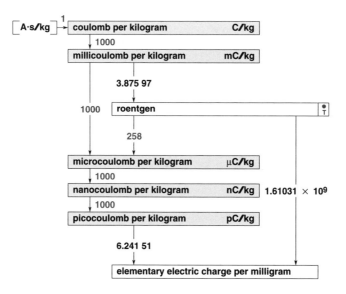

ABSORBED DOSE (D)

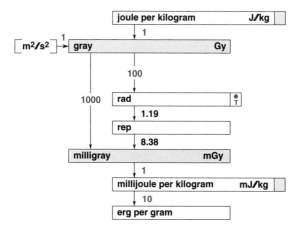

Example: Express 200 rep in terms of joules per kilogram

Solution: 200 rep = 200 ($\times$ 8.38) ($\div$ 1000) ($\div$ 1) J/kg = 1.68 J/kg

TEMPERATURE (T, t)

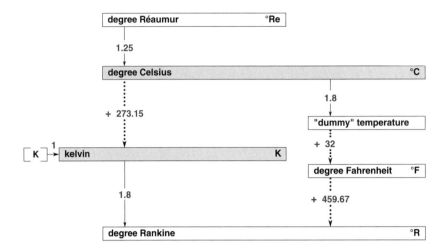

Note: Celsius was formerly called centigrade

The «dummy» temperature is simply a convenient interface between °F and °C

In dotted lines: with the arrow ADD; against the arrow SUBSTRACT

Examples of temperature conversion:

80 degrees Réaumur	=	80 (× 1.25) °C = 100 °C
100 degrees Celsius	=	(100 + 273.15) K = 373.15 K
100 degrees Celsius	=	100 (× 1.8) + 32°F = 212°F
108 degrees Fahrenheit	=	(108 + 459.67) ÷ 1.8 K = 567.67 (÷ 1.8) K = 315.372 K

TEMPERATURE INTERVAL (T, t, θ)

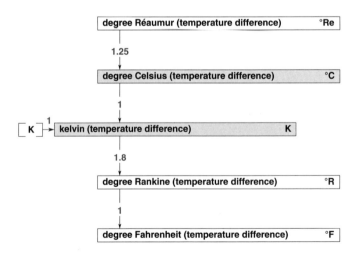

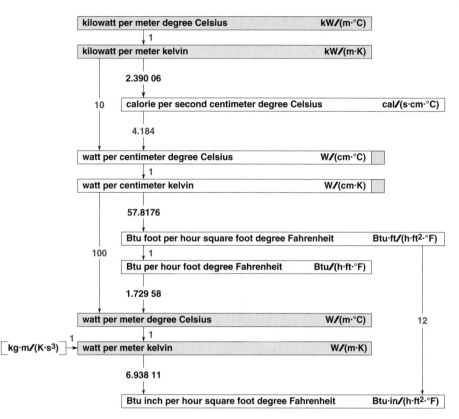

Note: the Btu and the calorie are defined in several ways (see pages 20, 21).
In this chart they are *thermochemical* units

Example: Convert 500 Btu/(h·ft·°F) into watts per meter kelvin
Solution: 500 Btu/(h·ft·°F) = 500 (× 1.729 58) (× 1) W/(m·K) = 864.79 W/(m·K)

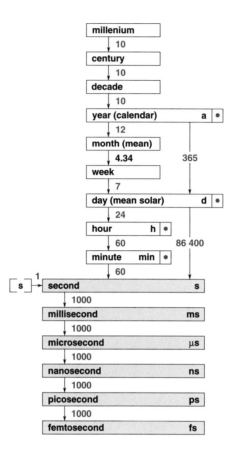

TORQUE (*T*)

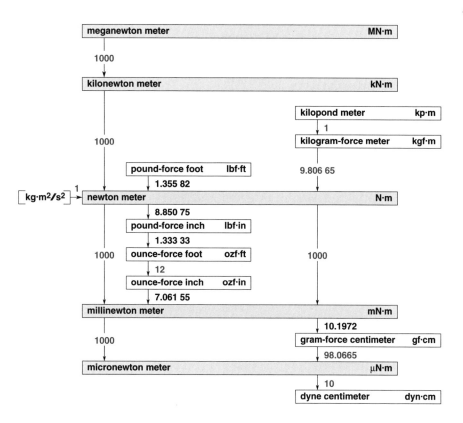

Example: Convert 12 000 pound-force foot to kilonewton meters

Solution: 12 000 lbf·ft = 12 000 (× 1.355 82) (÷ 1000) kN·m = 16.2698 kN·m

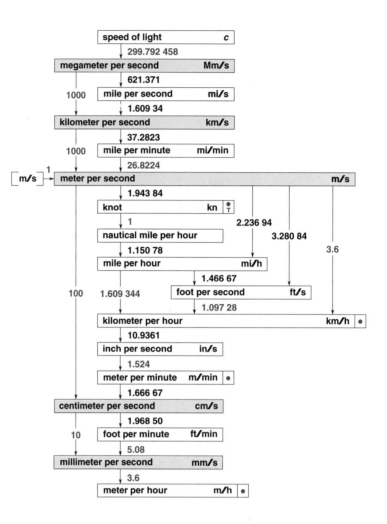

Example: Convert 75 meters per second into miles per hour

Solution: 75 m/s = 75 (× 2.236 94) mi/h = 167.77 mi/h

VISCOSITY

DYNAMIC VISCOSITY (η)

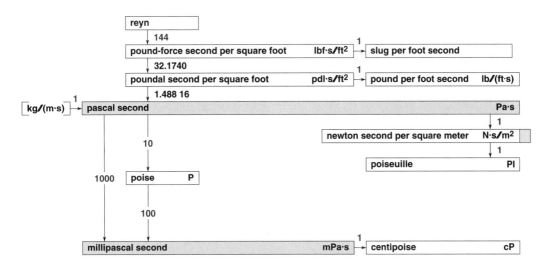

KINEMATIC VISCOSITY (ν)

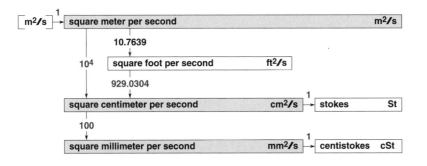

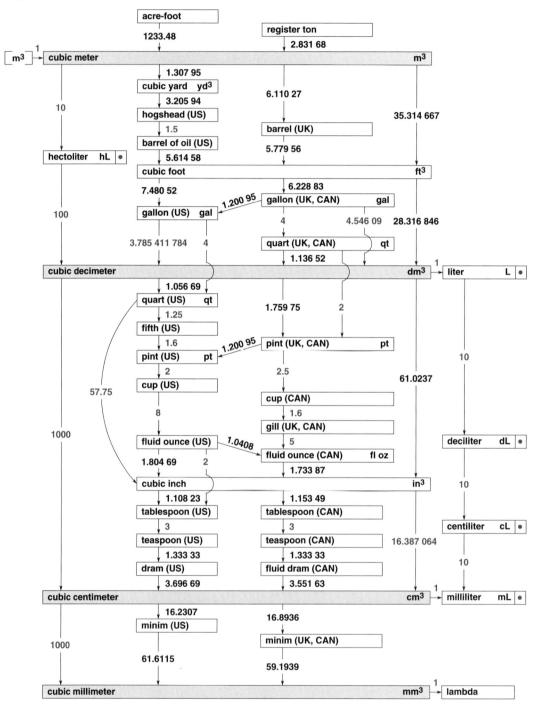

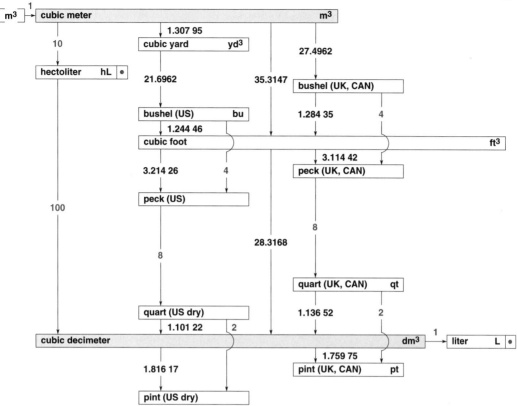

Note: SI units of volume make no distinction between liquid capacity and dry capacity.
   (UK, CAN) stands for United Kingdom, Canada.

Example: Convert 5000 cubic feet to cubic meters

Solution: 5000 ft^3 = 5000 (÷ 35.3147) m^3 = 141.584 m^3

SELECTED PHYSICAL CONSTANTS

Quantity	Quoted Value	S*	SI Unit	Symbol
Atomic mass constant	$1.660\,5402 \times 10^{-27}$	10	kg	m_u
Avogadro constant	$6.022\,1367 \times 10^{23}$	36	mol^{-1}	N_A
Bohr magneton	$9.274\,0154 \times 10^{-24}$	31	$J{\cdot}T^{-1}$	μ_B
Boltzmann constant	$1.380\,658 \times 10^{-23}$	12	$J{\cdot}K^{-1}$	$k\,(= R/N_A)$
Electron charge	$1.602\,177\,33 \times 10^{-19}$	49	C	$-e$
Electron specific charge	$-1.758\,819\,62 \times 10^{11}$	53	$C{\cdot}kg^{-1}$	$-e/m_e$
Electron rest mass	$9.109\,3897 \times 10^{-31}$	54	kg	m_e
Faraday constant	$9.648\,5309 \times 10^4$	29	$C{\cdot}mol^{-1}$	F
Fine-structure constant	$0.007\,297\,353\,08$	33	–	α
Josephson frequency to voltage ratio	$4.835\,9767 \times 10^{14}$	14	$Hz{\cdot}V^{-1}$	$2e/h$
Magnetic flux quantum	$2.067\,834\,61 \times 10^{-15}$	61	Wb	ϕ_o
Molar gas constant	$8.314\,510$	70	$J{\cdot}mol^{-1}{\cdot}K^{-1}$	R
Newtonian gravitational constant	$6.672\,59 \times 10^{-11}$	85	$m^3{\cdot}kg^{-1}{\cdot}s^{-2}$	G
Permeability of vacuum	$4\pi \times 10^{-7}$	d	H/m	μ_o
Permittivity of vacuum	$8.854\,1878\cdots \times 10^{-12}$	d	F/m	ε_o
Planck constant	$6.626\,0755 \times 10^{-34}$	40	$J{\cdot}s$	h
Planck constant/2π	$1.054\,572\,66 \times 10^{-34}$	63	$J{\cdot}s$	$\hbar\,(= h/2\pi)$
Quantum of circulation	$3.636\,948\,07 \times 10^{-4}$	33	$J{\cdot}s{\cdot}kg^{-1}$	$h/2m_e$
Rydberg constant	$1.097\,373\,1534 \times 10^7$	13	m^{-1}	R_∞
Standard volume of ideal gas	$22.414\,10 \times 10^{-3}$	19	$m^3{\cdot}mol^{-1}$	V_m
Stefan-Boltzmann constant	$5.670\,51 \times 10^{-8}$	19	$W{\cdot}K^{-4}{\cdot}m^{-2}$	σ
Speed of light	$299\,792\,458$	d	$m{\cdot}s^{-1}$	c

* The numbers in this column are the one-standard-deviation uncertainties in the last digits of the quoted value. The symbol **d** stands here for defined value.

Drawn from E.R. Cohen and B.N. Taylor "The 1986 Adjustment of the Fundamental Physical Constants", Committee on Data for Science and Technology (CODATA) Bulletin Number 63, November 1986.

2

THE INTERNATIONAL SYSTEM OF UNITS

In 1960, at the Eleventh General Conference of Weights and Measures held at Sèvres, France, a world system of units was established, officially named "Système international d'unités". The International System of Units is universally designated by the abbreviation SI.

2.1 Base and Derived Units of the SI

The foundation of the International System of Units rests upon seven base quantities: length, mass, time, electric current, temperature, luminous intensity and amount of substance. In turn, they give rise to seven base units: the meter, the kilogram, the second, the ampere, the kelvin, the candela and the mole. These quantities and their SI units are listed in Table 2-1.

TABLE 2-1	BASE UNITS OF THE SI	
Quantity	unit name	symbol of unit
Length	meter	m
Mass	kilogram	kg
Time	second	s
Electric current	ampere	A
Temperature	kelvin	K
Luminous intensity	candela	cd
Amount of substance	mole	mol

From these base units, other units are derived to express physical quantities such as area, power, force, magnetic flux, and so forth. Some of these derived units occur so frequently that they have been given special names. These special names are listed in Table 2-2.

TABLE 2 - 2	DERIVED UNITS AND SUPPLEMENTARY UNITS WITH SPECIAL NAMES		

Quantity	unit name	symbol of unit	formula of unit
Absorbed dose	gray	Gy	J/kg
Activity (radionuclide)	becquerel	Bq	1/s
Capacitance	farad	F	C/V
Celsius temperature (interval)	degree Celsius	°C	K
Dose equivalent	sievert	Sv	J/kg
Electric charge	coulomb	C	A·s
Electric conductance	siemens	S	$1/\Omega$
Electric potential	volt	V	W/A
Electric resistance	ohm	Ω	V/A
Energy, work	joule	J	N·m
Force	newton	N	$kg·m/s^2$
Frequency	hertz	Hz	1/s
Illuminance	lux	lx	$cd·sr/m^2$
Inductance	henry	H	Wb/A
Luminous flux	lumen	lm	cd·sr
Magnetic flux	weber	Wb	V·s
Magnetic flux density	tesla	T	Wb/m^2
Power	watt	W	J/s
Pressure, stress	pascal	Pa	N/m^2

Supplementary Units*			
Plane angle	radian	rad	$1 (= m/m)$
Solid angle	steradian	sr	$1 (= m^2/m^2)$

* In 1980 the Comité international des poids et mesures (CIPM) decided to interpret the class of supplementary units in the International System as a class of derived units.

Only those symbols of units that are named after an individual are capitalized.

2.2 Definitions of SI Base Units

The **meter** (m) is the length of the path travelled by light in vacuum during a time interval of 1/299 792 458 of a second.

The **kilogram** (kg) is the unit of mass; it is equal to the mass of the international prototype of the kilogram. *(The international prototype, made of platinum-iridium (90% platinum, 10% iridium) is preserved in a vault at Sèvres, France, by the International Bureau of Weights and Measures under conditions specified by the 1st CGPM in 1889. The prototype is a cylinder about 4 cm high and 4 cm in diameter).*

The **second** (s) is the duration of 9 192 631 770 periods of the radiation corresponding to the transition between the two hyperfine levels of the ground state of the cesium-133 atom.

The **ampere** (A) is that constant current which, if maintained in two straight parallel conductors of infinite length, of negligible circular cross section, and placed 1 meter apart in vacuum, would produce between these conductors a force equal to 2×10^{-7} newton per meter of length.

The **kelvin** (K), unit of thermodynamic temperature, is the fraction 1/273.16 of the thermodynamic temperature of the triple point of water.

The **candela** (cd) is the luminous intensity, in a given direction, of a source that emits monochromatic radiation of frequency 540×10^{12} hertz and that has a radiant intensity in that direction of 1/683 watt per steradian.

The **mole** (mol) is the amount of substance of a system which contains as many elementary entities as there are atoms in 0.012 kilogram of carbon 12. *Note:* When the mole is used, the elementary entities must be specified and may be atoms, molecules, ions, electrons, other particles, or specified groups of such particles.

2.3 Definitions of Supplementary Units

The **radian** (rad) is the angle between two radii of a circle which cuts off on the circumference an arc equal in length to the radius.

The **steradian** (sr) is the solid angle which, having its vertex in the center of a sphere, cuts off an area of the surface of the sphere equal to that of a square with sides of length equal to the radius of the sphere.

2.4 Definitions of Derived Units with special names

The derived units are defined as follows:

The **becquerel** (Bq) is the activity of a radionuclide decaying at the rate of one spontaneous nuclear transition per second.

The **coulomb** (C) is the quantity of electricity transported in 1 second by a current of 1 ampere. *(Hence 1 coulomb = 1 ampere second)*

The **degree Celsius** (°C) is used for expressing Celsius temperature (symbol t) defined by the equation $t = T - T_0$ where T is the thermodynamic temperature in kelvins and $T_0 = 273.15$ K, by definition. A temperature *interval* of 1 degree Celsius is therefore equal to a temperature interval of 1 kelvin.

The **farad** (F) is the capacitance of a capacitor between the plates of which there appears a difference of potential of 1 volt when it is charged by a quantity of electricity equal to 1 coulomb. *(Hence 1 farad = 1 coulomb per volt)*

The **gray** (Gy) is the absorbed dose when the energy per unit mass imparted to matter by ionizing radiation is one joule per kilogram. *Note:* The gray is also used for the ionizing radiation quantities: specific energy imparted, kerma, and absorbed dose index.

The **henry** (H) is the inductance of a closed circuit in which an electromotive force of 1 volt is produced when the electric current in the circuit varies uniformly at a rate of 1 ampere per second. *(Hence 1 henry = 1 volt second per ampere)*

The **hertz** (Hz) is the frequency of a periodic phenomenon of which the period is 1 second. *(Hence 1 hertz = 1 per second)*

The **joule** (J) is the work done when the point of application of 1 newton is displaced a distance of 1 meter in the direction of the force. *(Hence 1 joule = 1 newton meter)*

The **lumen** (lm) is the luminous flux emitted in a solid angle of 1 steradian by a uniform point source having an intensity of 1 candela. *(Hence 1 lumen = 1 candela steradian)*

The **lux** (lx) is the unit of illuminance equal to one lumen per square meter.

The **newton** (N) is that force which gives to a mass of 1 kilogram an acceleration of 1 meter per second per second. *(Hence 1 newton = 1 kilogram meter per second squared)*

The **ohm** (Ω) is the electric resistance between two points of a conductor when a constant difference of potential of 1 volt, applied between these two points, produces in this conductor a current of 1 ampere, this conductor not being the source of any electromotive force. *(Hence 1 ohm = 1 volt per ampere)*

The **pascal** (Pa) is the unit of pressure or stress equal to one newton per square meter.

The **siemens** (S) is the unit of electric conductance equal to one reciprocal ohm.

The **sievert** (Sv) is the dose equivalent when the absorbed dose of ionizing radiation multiplied by the dimensionless factors Q (quality factor) and N (product of any other multiplying factors) stipulated by the International Commission on Radiological Protection is one joule per kilogram.

The **tesla** (T) is the unit of magnetic flux density equal to one weber per square meter.

The **volt** (V) is the difference of electric potential between two points of a conducting wire carrying a constant current of 1 ampere, when the power dissipated between these points is equal to 1 watt. *(Hence 1 volt = 1 watt per ampere)*

The **watt** (W) is the power which gives rise to the production of energy at the rate of 1 joule per second. *(Hence 1 watt = 1 joule per second)*

The **weber** (Wb) is the magnetic flux which, linking a circuit of one turn, produces in it an electromotive force of 1 volt as it is reduced to zero at a uniform rate in 1 second. *(Hence 1 weber = 1 volt second)*

2.5 Multiples and submultiples

We have seen that the magnitude of a quantity can cover a tremendous range, from the infinitesimally small to the extremely large. To accommodate this range, it is convenient to define multiples and submultiples of the SI unit that would otherwise be used to measure the quantity. To create these multiples and submultiples, the SI has assigned 20 prefixes. They multiply the SI unit by factors ranging from 10^{24} to 10^{-24}. These prefixes and their symbols are shown in Table 2-3. Using this prefix designation, a length of 1000 meters is called a *kilo*meter, while

TABLE 2 - 3		MULTIPLES AND SUBMULTIPLES OF SI UNITS	
prefix	multiplier	symbol	example
yotta	10^{24}	Y	$4 \text{ Y}\Omega = 4 \text{ yottaohms} = 4 \times 10^{24} \, \Omega$
zetta	10^{21}	Z	$5 \text{ Zm} = 5 \text{ zettameters} = 5 \times 10^{21} \text{ m}$
exa	10^{18}	E	$2 \text{ E}\Omega = 2 \text{ exaohms} = 2 \times 10^{18} \, \Omega$
peta	10^{15}	P	$3 \text{ PJ} = 3 \text{ petajoules} = 3 \times 10^{15} \text{ J}$
tera	10^{12}	T	$4 \text{ TW} = 4 \text{ terawatts} = 4 \times 10^{12} \text{ W}$
giga	10^{9}	G	$5 \text{ GW·h} = 5 \text{ gigawatthours} = 5 \times 10^{9} \text{ W·h}$
mega	10^{6}	M	$6 \text{ MPa} = 6 \text{ megapascals} = 6 \times 10^{6} \text{ Pa}$
kilo	10^{3}	k	$7 \text{ km} = 7 \text{ kilometers} = 7000 \text{ m}$
hecto	100	h	$8 \text{ hL} = 8 \text{ hectoliters} = 800 \text{ L}$
deka	10	da	$9 \text{ dam} = 9 \text{ decameters} = 90 \text{ m}$
deci	1/10	d	$3 \text{ dm}^3 = 3 \text{ cubic decimeters} = 3 \times (0.1 \text{ m})^3 = 0.003 \text{ m}^3$
centi	1/100	c	$2 \text{ cm} = 2 \text{ centimeters} = (2/100) \text{ m} = 0.02 \text{ m}$
milli	10^{-3}	m	$3 \text{ mV} = 3 \text{ millivolts} = 3 \times 10^{-3} \text{ V}$
micro	10^{-6}	µ	$4 \, \mu\text{F} = 4 \text{ microfarads} = 4 \times 10^{-6} \text{ F}$
nano	10^{-9}	n	$5 \text{ ns} = 5 \text{ nanoseconds} = 5 \times 10^{-9} \text{ s}$
pico	10^{-12}	p	$6 \text{ pA} = 6 \text{ picoamperes} = 6 \times 10^{-12} \text{ A}$
femto	10^{-15}	f	$7 \text{ fm} = 7 \text{ femtometers} = 7 \times 10^{-15} \text{ m}$
atto	10^{-18}	a	$8 \text{ aJ} = 8 \text{ attojoules} = 8 \times 10^{-18} \text{ J}$
zepto	10^{-21}	z	$7 \text{ zm} = 7 \text{ zeptometers} = 7 \times 10^{-21} \text{ m}$
yocto	10^{-24}	y	$9 \text{ yJ} = 9 \text{ yoctojoules} = 9 \times 10^{-24} \text{ J}$

ONE PART IN ONE MILLION

Knowing that some quantities can be measured to one part in 100 million, we are sometimes inclined to believe that an accuracy of one part in one million is rather routine. This could not be farther from the truth. Such accuracy requires the combined knowledge and experience of highly competent scientists and technicians, who must have a thorough understanding of optics, electronics, mathematics, thermodynamics, mechanics and molecular physics and must possess the engineering know-how to build the equipment and make it work. Few industrial projects require as wide a range of knowledge as does the measurement of one of the basic physical standards.

An accuracy of one part in one million is a great achievement. It commands respect, for to improve it by a factor of 10 always requires a new approach, generally made possible only by a major advance in technology.

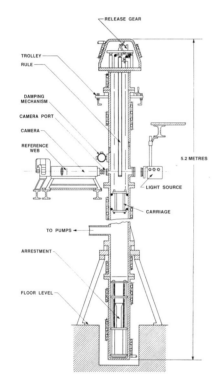

For example, in the determination of the acceleration due to gravity*, a 2-meter rule was dropped from a height of 5.2 m inside an evacuated column, and its position was photographed at 0.1 second intervals using a pulsed light source and a camera, as shown in the accompanying diagram. Knowing the time t and position s (distance) it is possible to calculate the acceleration g due to gravity (to a first approximation) from the formula $g = 2s/t^2$.

This looks like a rather simple problem, and indeed it is - unless you are looking for an accuracy of 1 part in 1 million. Then everything becomes important, and nothing must be overlooked.

Some of the problems which were encountered in this free fall experiment, and how they were solved, illustrate the time, thought and ingenuity which must be employed in all precise measurements of physical quantities (see facing page).

* Details adapted from **"An Absolute Measurement of the Acceleration due to Gravity at Ottawa"** (1960), by H. Preston-Thomas, L.G. Turnbull, E. Green, T.M. Dauphinee and S.N. Karla. National Research Council of Canada, Division of Physics, NRC No 5693.

PROBLEM	SOLUTION
1. The length of the rule must be known to better than 1 part per million (1 ppm).	Calibrate the rule against the standard metre using optical interference techniques.
2. Time must be known to better than 1 ppm.	Use a quartz crystal oscillator as a base source; its frequency is known to 2 parts in 1000 million.
3. Air causes viscous drag.	Design and build a 5.2 meter column, place the rule inside and reduce pressure to less than 80 micropascals by vacuum diffusion pumps.
4. The length of the rule changes with temperature.	Keep the temperature within 0.004 °C over the length of the rule and stabilize it by a) keeping the column temperature to within 0.05°C over its 5.2 m height by tempera-ture - equalizing water coils and b) enclosing the rule in a radiation shield.
5. The earth's magnetic field will produce eddy currents in the moving metallic rule, which will slow its rate of fall.	Use non-magnetic stainless steel and place degaussing coils around the column to reduce the magnetism to negligible levels.
6. Owing to its weight, the rule stretches when it hangs from its pivot, and is therefore longer than when it was calibrated.	Take photographs after the rule is released and only after it has had time to return to its calibrated length.
7. Small vibrations and earth tremors could misalign the optical axes. Tremors must be less than one millionth of a metre.	a) Install 3 seismographs around the camera to evaluate the magnitude of the tremors. b) Mount camera and light source on separate, heavy, I-beam supports.
8. The rule expands in a vacuum.	Determine the stress/strain properties of the rule and apply correction.
9. Light shining on the rule will produce local heating.	Place infrared filters in the path of the beam and focus as quickly as possible.
10. The weight of the rule increases as it falls, and this affects the acceleration.	Make mathematical analysis and apply correction.
11. Air molecules which remain in the column obstruct the descent of the rule.	Conduct a series of tests at various degrees of vacuum, correlate results with the momentum of molecules, and apply correction.

1/1000 of a meter (0.001 meter) is called a *milli*meter. Similarly, 1/10 of a liter is called one *deci*liter and 100 liters is one *hecto*liter.

However, in the interest of simplicity, and to minimize the possibilities of error, the prefixes centi, deca, deci and hecto are often avoided. For example, machine-tool manufacturers commonly quote lengths only in meters and millimeters.

2.6 Standards

In a measurement system, the base units are essentially *definitions* of physical quantities, and so they are absolutely exact. Base units are duplicated in the real world by *standards* which are the physical embodiment of the base units. These standards can approach the defined values of the base units very closely. However, because the standards are affected by temperature, pressure and other extraneous variables, they approach the base unit with high accuracy only under prescribed conditions. Typical accuracies that are attainable in standards laboratories for SI base units are listed below.

kilogram : 1 part in 10^8 meter : 1 part in 10^{10} second: 1 part in 10^{13}

ampere :   1 part in 10^6 kelvin : 1 part in 10^6 candela : 1 part in 10^3

mole :   1 part in 10^6

The insert on page 54 gives some indication of the expertise and meticulous care that was needed to achieve an accuracy of one part in one million. Owing to advances in technology, the accuracy of measurement of the acceleration due to gravity has since been improved by a factor of 100.

REVIEW QUESTIONS

2.1   Name the seven base quantities of the International System of Units.

2.2   Name the seven base units of the SI.

2.3   Give the symbols of the seven base units, with particular attention to capitalization.

2.4   Give the SI definition of the unit of force and of the unit of mass.

2.5   What are the SI units of force, pressure, energy, plane angle, power and frequency? Give their symbols, paying particular attention to capitalization.

2.6   Give the appropriate prefix for the following multipliers: 100, 1000, 10^6, 1/10, 1/100, 1/1000, 10^{-6}, 10^{-9}.

Express the following multiples and submultiples of SI units in symbol form

2.7 millipascal	2.13 milligram	2.19 nanosecond
2.8 terajoule	2.14 kilomole	2.20 picofarad
2.9 megapascal	2.15 milliwatt	2.21 picoampere
2.10 kilohertz	2.16 milliradian	2.22 kilovolt
2.11 megohm	2.17 kilonewton	2.23 kilometer
2.12 centimeter	2.18 millitesla	2.24 microweber

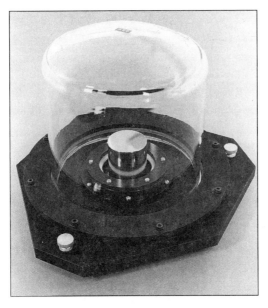

Primary platinum-iridium kilogram standard. (*Courtesy NIST*)

NIST-7 is the cesium-beam primary frequency standard for for the United States. At an accuracy of 1×10^{-14}, this standard contributes significantly to the accuracy of the rate of international time and lends long-term stability to NIST's time scale. This increased stability is needed for large network applications and for tests of scientific theories. The standard also serves as a reference in evaluating the performance of advanced commercial frequency standards. (*Courtesy of NIST,* the National Institute of Standards and Technology, United States Department of Commerce.)

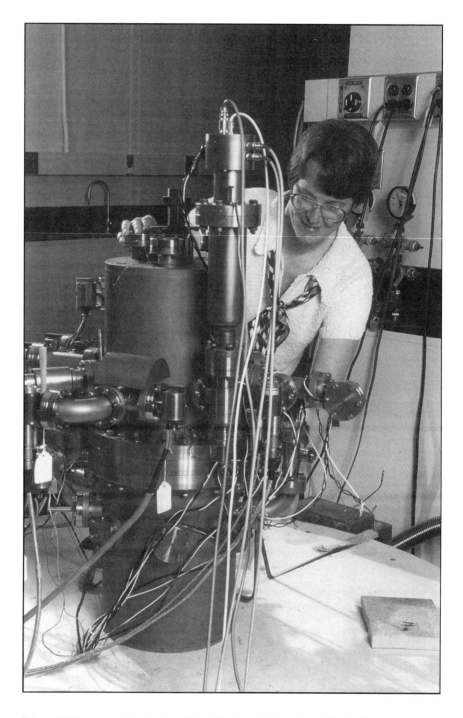

Primary high vacuum standard used to calibrate spinning rotor and ionization gages.
(*Courtesy NIST*)

3

THE CONVERSION PROCESS

Owing to the existence of various systems of measurement, such as the English system, the U.S. Customary system, the older metric systems and the modern SI, it often happens that a physical quantity is expressed in units that do not correspond to the units we want to use. For example, if the pressure in a tire is given in pounds-force per square inch, we may want to know what it is in terms of kilopascals. In such cases, it is important to follow a conversion method that leaves no room for doubt as to the correctness of the result.

3.1 Ratios of units

The magnitude of a physical quantity is always expressed as the product of a *number* times a *unit.* For example, the time to hold one's breath can be expressed as $t = 37$ seconds, meaning t (a *quantity*) $= 37$ (a *number*) $\times$ second (a *unit*). Using the SI symbol for second, this can be expressed as $t = 37$ s.

In the formal treatment of quantities and units (and using the ISO brace{ } and bracket [ ] notation), the relationship may be expressed in the form

$$Q = \{N\}\,[U]$$

where Q is the symbol for the quantity, [U] the symbol for the unit, and {N} symbolizes the numerical value of the quantity Q expressed in the unit [U]. However, when the meaning is clear, the numerical values and the unit symbols are usually shown without the braces and brackets.

When converting a quantity from one unit to another, it is important to understand that the symbol of a unit (or even its name) can be treated like an algebraic symbol. We can divide, multiply, substitute, or take the square root of a unit, as the need may arise.

Consider, for example, two units of length: the centimeter and the inch. One inch is exactly 2.54 times as long as one centimeter and so the inch is clearly bigger than the centimeter. We can express the ratio of these two units (or their symbols) by

$$\frac{\text{inch}}{\text{centimeter}} = \frac{2.54}{1} = 2.54 \quad \text{or simply} \quad \frac{\text{in}}{\text{cm}} = 2.54$$

and, by inverting,

$$\frac{\text{cm}}{\text{in}} = \frac{1}{2.54} \approx 0.393\,700\,787$$

Using the rules of algebra, we can also transpose the units to produce the result: in = 2.54 cm. Thus, if desired, we can substitute inch by the quantity 2.54 cm.

The ratio of two units that belong to the same physical quantity can always be expressed as a number. Thus, the ratio quart/cubic meter can be expressed as a number because both units belong to the same family of physical quantities, namely, volume.

In summary:

1) The symbols (and names) of units can be treated like algebraic symbols.

2) The ratio of two units of a given physical quantity always yields a pure number.

The conversion charts enable us to find the numerical value of the ratio of two units very easily. Starting with the unit in the numerator, we simply follow the arrows leading to the unit in the denominator. In so doing, we observe the usual rule: with the arrow *multiply*, against the arrow *divide*.

The following examples show how these ratios are determined, with the values drawn from the respective conversion charts.

$$\frac{\text{pound-force}}{\text{newton}} = 4.448\ 22 \quad \text{(page 24)}$$

$$\frac{\text{pound}}{\text{kilogram}} = (\times 453.592\ 37)(\div 1000) = 0.453\ 592\ 37 \quad \text{(exact value, page 30)}$$

$$or \quad \frac{\text{pound}}{\text{kilogram}} = (\div 2.204\ 62) = 0.453\ 593 \quad \text{(approximate value, page 30)}$$

$$\frac{\text{bar}}{\text{atmosphere}} = (\times 1.019\ 72)(\times 98.0665)(\div 101.325) = 0.986\ 927 \quad \text{(page 37)}$$

$$\frac{\text{square foot}}{\text{hectare}} = (\div 43\ 560)(\div 2.471\ 05) = \frac{1}{107\ 639} = 9.290\ 32 \times 10^{-6} \quad \text{(page 12)}$$

From the above, it is also clear that the ratio of a unit to itself yields the simple number 1. Thus:

$$\frac{\text{kilometer}}{\text{kilometer}} = 1 \qquad \frac{\text{newton}}{\text{newton}} = 1 \qquad \frac{\text{pound}}{\text{pound}} = 1 \quad \text{and so forth.}$$

The number 1 can therefore be used to signify the ratio of two identical units. We will now make use of this fact.

3.2 Converting units

We can convert the units of a physical quantity into other units by using the so-called ratio technique. For example, suppose we want to convert a mass of 15 pounds into kilograms. We proceed as follows:

15 pounds = 15 lb
$$= 15 \text{ lb} \times 1$$

The one "1" after 15 lb prepares the entry for the unit we want to convert to, namely the kilogram, as shown below:

$$15 \text{ pounds} = 15 \text{ lb} \times \frac{\text{unit we want to convert to}}{\text{unit we want to convert to}}$$

$$= 15 \text{ lb} \times \frac{\text{kg}}{\text{kg}}$$

Next, we shift the unit in the denominator, thus creating the ratio lb / kg:

$$15 \text{ pounds} = 15 \; \frac{\text{lb}}{\text{kg}} \times \text{kg}$$

Recalling that lb / kg has a value of 0.453 592 37, we can write:

$$15 \text{ pounds} = 15 \times 0.453 \ 592 \ 37 \text{ kg}$$

$$= 6.8039 \text{ kg}$$

We thus find that 15 pounds is equal to 6.8039 kilograms.

As another example, let us convert 25 meters into yards, knowing the value of the following ratios:

meter/centimeter = 100; foot/inch = 12; yard/foot = 3; inch/centimeter =2.54

In this case, we do not have the direct conversion factor linking meter and yard, and so we use *intermediate ratios* to arrive at the result. We proceed as follows:

$$25 \text{ meters} = 25 \text{ meter} \times 1 \times 1 \times 1 \times \frac{\text{unit we want to convert to}}{\text{unit we want to convert to}}$$

The three 1's in the above expression represent the ratio of any identical units of length that are pertinent to our problem, namely inch/inch, centimeter/centimeter, and foot/foot. Using these intermediate units, we can write:

$$25 \text{ meters} = 25 \times \text{meter} \times \frac{\text{centimeter}}{\text{centimeter}} \times \frac{\text{inch}}{\text{inch}} \times \frac{\text{foot}}{\text{foot}} \times \frac{\text{yard}}{\text{yard}}$$

Next, by shifting the units in the denominator, we obtain four known ratios which enable us to calculate the result:

$$25 \text{ meters} = 25 \times \frac{\text{meter}}{\text{centimeter}} \times \frac{\text{centimeter}}{\text{inch}} \times \frac{\text{inch}}{\text{foot}} \times \frac{\text{foot}}{\text{yard}} \times \text{yard}$$

$$= 25 \times 100 \times \frac{1}{2.54} \times \frac{1}{12} \times \frac{1}{3} \times \text{yard}$$

$$= 27.34 \times \text{yard}$$

$$= 27.34 \text{ yd}$$

From the above examples, we can now deduce a general equation that permits us to convert a quantity expressed in a given unit U_{given} into one having the desired unit $U_{desired}$:

$$Q = \text{magnitude of the quantity}$$

$$= \{\text{numerical value}\} \times [\text{given unit}]$$

$$= N_{given} \times U_{given}$$

$$= N_{given} \times U_{given} \times \frac{U_1}{U_1} \times \frac{U_2}{U_2} \times \ldots \times \frac{U_n}{U_n} \times \frac{U_{desired}}{U_{desired}}$$

and so

$$Q = N_{given} \times \frac{U_{given}}{U_1} \times \frac{U_1}{U_2} \times \frac{U_2}{U_3} \times \ldots \times \frac{U_n}{U_{desired}} \times U_{desired} \qquad (3\text{-}1)$$

in which

Q = magnitude of the physical quantity, composed of a number times a unit

U_{given} = given unit

$U_{desired}$ = desired unit

$U_1, U_2, U_3, \ldots U_n$ = intermediate units (as required)

This successive multiplication process, revealed in equation (3-1), is at the root of the conversion methodology used in the conversion charts. In effect, as we move along an arrowed path, starting from U_{given}, we successively multiply the ratios of the units we meet, until we reach $U_{desired}$.

3.3 Compound units

The same procedure can be used to convert quantities that involve compound units, such as converting miles per hour into meters per second. Indeed, let us convert 60 mi/h into m/s, knowing the following conversion factors:

1 mi = 5280 ft, 1 h = 3600 s, 1 ft = 12 in, 1 in = 2.54 cm, 1 m = 100 cm.

The calculations on the next page illustrate the procedure step by step. To better understand the methodology, the reader is invited to examine the individual steps. Note, in particular, that we can transpose the symbols of units as if they were algebraic symbols. We can also substitute a unit by its equivalent magnitude, such as in rows four and five where mi is replaced by 5280 ft.

Of course, if the VELOCITY chart on page 44 is used, the answer to the above example is obtained immediately: 60 mi/h ($\div$ 2.236 94) = 26.8224 m/s.

60 miles per hour = 60 miles per hour × $\dfrac{\text{unit we want to convert to}}{\text{unit we want to convert to}}$

$$= 60 \times \frac{\text{mi}}{\text{h}} \times \frac{\text{m/s}}{\text{m/s}}$$

$$= 60 \times \frac{\text{mi}}{\text{h}} \times \frac{\text{s}}{\text{m}} \times \text{m/s} \quad \text{(rearrange terms)}$$

$$= 60 \times \frac{\text{mi}}{\text{m}} \times \frac{\text{s}}{\text{h}} \times \text{m/s} \quad \text{(create ratios of similar units)}$$

$$= 60 \times \frac{5280 \text{ ft}}{\text{m}} \times \frac{1}{3600} \times \text{m/s}$$

$$= 60 \times \frac{\text{ft}}{\text{m}} \times \frac{5280}{3600} \times \text{m/s}$$

$$= 60 \times \frac{12 \text{ in}}{\text{m}} \times \frac{5280}{3600} \times \text{m/s}$$

$$= 60 \times \frac{\text{in}}{\text{m}} \times \frac{12 \times 5280}{3600} \times \text{m/s}$$

$$= 60 \times \frac{2.54 \text{ cm}}{\text{m}} \times \frac{12 \times 5280}{3600} \times \text{m/s}$$

$$= 60 \times \frac{2.54}{100} \times \frac{12 \times 5280}{3600} \times \text{m/s}$$

$$= 26.8224 \text{ m/s}$$

3.4 Chain method of conversion

Instead of the above laborious conversion procedure, the main purpose of which is to illustrate how units can be manipulated and transposed, we can use the so-called chain method. This popular method of conversion arranges the units in pairs so that their ratio is equal to 1. For example, knowing that 1 ft = 12 in, we can write [12 in/ft] = 1, or alternatively [ft/12 in] =1. Similarly, knowing that 1 calorie = 4.184 J, we obtain the unity ratios [cal/4.184 J] =1, or [4.184 J/cal] =1.

The quantity we want to convert can be successively multiplied by such unity ratios without in any way altering its magnitude. The trick is to select unity ratios that contain units that will successively cancel out, until we are left with the units we want. Using the chain method in the example of Section 3.3, we can readily convert 60 mi/h to meters per second, as follows:

$$60 \text{ mi/h} = 60 \times \frac{\text{mi}}{\text{h}} \times \left[\frac{5280 \text{ ft}}{\text{mi}} \right] \times \left[\frac{12 \text{ in}}{\text{ft}} \right] \times \left[\frac{2.54 \text{ cm}}{\text{in}} \right] \times \left[\frac{\text{m}}{100 \text{ cm}} \right] \times \left[\frac{\text{h}}{3600 \text{ s}} \right]$$

cancelling units, we obtain:

$$60 \text{ mi/h} = 60 \times \frac{\cancel{\text{mi}}}{\cancel{\text{h}}} \times \left[\frac{5280 \cancel{\text{ft}}}{\cancel{\text{mi}}} \right] \times \left[\frac{12 \cancel{\text{in}}}{\cancel{\text{ft}}} \right] \times \left[\frac{2.54 \cancel{\text{cm}}}{\cancel{\text{in}}} \right] \times \left[\frac{\text{m}}{100 \cancel{\text{cm}}} \right] \times \left[\frac{\cancel{\text{h}}}{3600 \text{ s}} \right]$$

$$= 26.8224 \text{ m/s}$$

This intuitive chain method is a quick and elegant way of making conversions. By committing to memory only a few unity ratios, it is possible to make many conversions without using a reference.

REVIEW QUESTIONS

Using the conversion charts, determine, to 5-figure accuracy, the numerical value of the following ratios:

3.1 $\dfrac{\text{meter}}{\text{foot}}$ 3.4 $\dfrac{\text{kilogram}}{\text{pound}}$ 3.7 $\dfrac{\text{joule}}{\text{calorie}}$

3.2 $\dfrac{\text{inch}}{\text{meter}}$ 3.5 $\dfrac{\text{newton}}{\text{pound-force}}$ 3.8 $\dfrac{\text{Btu/min}}{\text{horsepower}}$

3.3 $\dfrac{\text{Btu}}{\text{joule}}$ 3.6 $\dfrac{\text{gallon (U.S.)}}{\text{liter}}$ 3.9 $\dfrac{\text{kilopascal}}{\text{atmosphere}}$

Using the ratio or the chain method, make the following conversions:

3.10   846 square millimeters to square inches

3.11   1 square mile to square kilometers

3.12   10 boiler horsepower to kilowatts

3.13   100 watts to calories per second

3.14   1200 foot pound-force per second to kilowatts

3.15   300 nanoamperes per square centimeter, to mA/m^2

3.16   120 kW·h to gigajoules

3.17   24 pounds-force to newtons

3.18   3 pounds-force to poundals

3.19   50 ounces (avdp) to kilograms

3.20   12 troy ounces to ounces (avdp)

3.21   3 metric tons (tonnes) to slugs

3.22   5000 meters to nautical miles

3.23   200 footcandles to lux

3.24   2 milligauss to teslas

3.25   2 quarts (Canadian) to fluid ounces (U.S.)

3.26   46 lb·ft^2 to kg·m^2

3.27   5 inches of water (60°F) to millimeters of mercury (0°C)

3.28   12 milliwebers to maxwells

3.29   1 revolution per year to microradians per second

3.30   25 radians per second to revolutions per minute

3.31   240 milligauss to microteslas

4

QUANTITY EQUATIONS

In dealing with scientific relationships it is important to distinguish between two types of equations: *quantity* equations and *numerical* equations. Both types are encountered in texts and reference books, and the concept of units and quantities is useful in understanding their respective features. In this chapter we cover the main features of quantities and quantity equations*.

4.1 Quantities

A quantity is any physical property that can be measured. We use several hundred quantities to describe and measure the physical world around us. A few of these quantities are listed below.

length	viscosity	area	electromotive force
time	energy	luminance	entropy
mass	speed	angle	pressure
force	power	temperature	momentum

A quantity may also be a physical constant, such as the gas constant, the Planck constant, or the rest mass of an electron.

4.2 Relationship between quantities

The study of physics is to a great extent the study of mathemetical relationships among various physical properties. When these properties allow a reasonable mathematical description, we define physical quantities, as above. By proper selection of a few *base quantities*, the relationship of all other quantities can be established in terms of these base quantities, either by definition, by geometry, by physical law, or by a combination of these three.

Pressure, for example, is a quantity that is related, by definition, to a quantity *force* divided by a quantity *area*. *Area*, in turn, is a quantity related, by geometry, to the product of two quantities of length. *Force*, on the other hand, is a quantity related, by Newton's second law, to the quantity *mass* times the quantity *acceleration*.

Even a seemingly isolated quantity such as *temperature* is related to the quantities *pressure*, *volume* and *mass* by virtue of the behavior of gases. We can even relate the quantities *length* and *time* by using that universal constant, the speed of light.

---

* Quantity equations are also called physical equations, or equations between quantities.
  Numerical equations are also called measure equations.

Thus, if we define our concepts correctly we can relate any quantity to any other by one or more of the three ways mentioned above.

The relationships between quantities are expressed in the form of *quantity equations*. Thus, the equation *area = length × width* is a quantity equation which states that the quantity (area of a rectangle) is equal to the quantity (length) times the quantity (width).

4.3 Base quantities

To deduce a set of quantity equations we must first establish a number of so-called *base* quantities. Base quantities are the building blocks upon which we erect the entire structure and relationships of the physical world. The number of base quantities, as well as their choice, is quite arbitrary but, in general, we try to select quantities that are easy to understand, that are frequently used and for which accurate, measurable standards can be set.

In this context, the International System of Units, or SI, makes use of seven base quantities: *mass, length, time, temperature, electric current, luminous intensity* and *amount of substance*.

4.4 Derived quantities

Derived quantities are those which can be deduced by definition, by geometry or by physical law, using the selected base quantities as building blocks. Examples of derived quantities are *velocity* (length/time), *area* (product of two lengths) and *force* (mass × acceleration).

4.5 Types of quantity equations

The energy in a hurricane, the pressure at the bottom of the sea, the weight of a stone and the viscosity of oil are physical quantities of nature which existed long before humans were on earth to measure them. And, whether they are measured or not, these quantities are there, interacting with each other according to fundamental laws. Because quantities – and not units – conform to the laws of nature, physicists often express these laws in terms of quantity equations.

Quantity equations possess two important features:

> 1. They show the relationship between quantities.

> 2. They can be used with any system of units.

There are three basic types of quantity equations:

> **1) Quantity equations established from the laws of nature;** example:

Newton's second law of motion

$$F = ma$$

in which
>> F = magnitude of the force
>> m = magnitude of the mass
>> a = magnitude of the acceleration

2) Quantity equations established from a definition; example:

definition of pressure

$$p = F/A$$

in which

p = magnitude of the pressure
F = magnitude of the force
A = magnitude of the area

3) Quantity equations arising from geometry; example:

Area of a circle

$$A = \pi r^2$$

in which

A = magnitude of the area
r = magnitude of the radius
π = coefficient based upon the geometry of a circle.

None of these equations imposes a particular set of units. Consequently, we are free to use any convenient units to describe the magnitudes of the quantities F, m, a, p, A and r.

Many quantity equations are a combination of the three basic types mentioned above, but in all cases we can use any units we please to describe the magnitudes of the physical quantities that are involved.

Some quantity equations contain a physical constant, such as the constant R_a in the equation giving the properties of dry air:

$$pV = R_a mT$$

in which

p = magnitude of the pressure
V = magnitude of the volume
R_a = magnitude of the constant for dry air = 287 J/(kg·K)
m = magnitude of the mass (of dry air)
T = magnitude of the absolute temperature

In this equation, the magnitude of R_a happens to be expressed in SI units, but this places no restriction on the units that may be used for the other four quantities p, V, m and T. Of course, the units must be compatible with the corresponding quantities.

How are quantity equations arrived at? The following sections describe how they are created.

4.6 Deducing a quantity equation

Whenever a new quantity is derived from a base quantity (such as mass, length or time), we try to establish a simple relationship, one in which the quantities are related in a one-to-one ratio. Let us, for example, find the quantity equation for *area*, given the base quantity of *length* (which may have any magnitude). To do so, we must first select a particular shape such as a triangle, an ellipse or a rectangle.

Let us choose a rectangle the length of whose sides are l and w, respectively. Simple geometry proves that the area A is proportional to the length times the width of the rectangle. Thus:

$$\text{area} \propto (\text{length}) \times (\text{width})$$

$$A \propto lw$$

or $\qquad A = klw$

In this expression, k is a constant which remains to be found. Now, l and w are base quantities of length, but the derived quantity "area" has not yet been defined. We can, therefore, assign to k any value we please, and the simplest choice is to let $k = 1$. We can then write $A = lw$ in which A, l and w represent the magnitudes of the quantities area, length and width. Note that no units are specified.

Having chosen a rectangle for our model, the expression $A = lw$ implies, tacitly, that this physical equation is correct for rectangles only. Suppose, for example, that we wish to find the physical equation for an ellipse whose major and minor axes have lengths l and w respectively. Simple geometry again tells us that the surface area S of the ellipse is proportional to $l \times w$, whence $S = k'lw$ where k' is some constant.

The question now arises, can we again let k' have any value at all? The answer is no, because we have already defined area in terms of a rectangle, so we can no longer assign to k' any value we please. Its value is determined by the geometry of the ellipse (as compared with that of a rectangle) and it can be shown that k' must equal $\pi/4$. Hence, for an ellipse the physical equation is $S = (\pi/4)lw$.

If we lived in a world where everything was round, we would probably have chosen an ellipse (instead of a rectangle) for our definition of area, with the result that a factor $4/\pi$ would appear in the areas of rectangles, triangles and squares – a most unusual state of affairs, but one which would be perfectly correct.

4.7 Deducing the quantity equation $F = ma$

Let us now deduce the quantity equation relating force, mass, and acceleration. According to Newton's second law of motion the acceleration a imparted to a body is directly proportional to the applied force F and inversely proportional to the mass m. This is expressed by the proportionality:

$$a \propto \frac{F}{m}$$

which may be cast into the more familiar form:

$$F \propto ma$$

which, in turn, can be written as an equation

$$F = kma$$

where k is some constant.

Now, in this equation, the mass m is a base quantity and the acceleration a is related to the base quantities length and time, but the quantity "force" has not yet been defined. We can, therefore, let k have any value we wish and the simplest choice is to let $k = 1$. This yields the quantity equation $F = ma$ which is the well-known expression for Newton's second law of motion.

4.8 The Law of Universal Gravitation

It often happens that quantities which are already related by virtue of some natural law, are found to be related by another equally important law. Such situations have to be treated with care, and the quantity equation for the Law of Universal Gravitation affords an excellent example.

According to this law, the force of attraction between two bodies is proportional to their masses m_1, m_2, and inversely proportional to the square of the distance d between their centers. This can be expressed by the proportionality:

$$F \propto \frac{m_1 m_2}{d^2}$$

which can be written as an equation:

$$F = G \frac{m_1 m_2}{d^2}$$

where G is some constant.

In this equation the masses m_1 and m_2 are base quantities and the distance d is also a base quantity. However, because the quantity F is already defined by virtue of Newton's second law, we can no longer assign to G any value we please. Its value can be determined only by experimental measurement and, to date, the value of G is known to be about 6.6732×10^{-11} m³/(kg·s²). The quantity equation which expresses the law of universal gravitation is therefore:

$$F = G \frac{m_1 m_2}{d^2}$$

in which $G = 6.672\ 59 \times 10^{-11}$ m³/(kg·s²) .

4.9 The coefficients of quantity equations

Many quantity equations are simple, possessing a coefficient of 1. Others, such as the quantity equation for the area of an ellipse, have exact numerical coefficients which depend upon geometry. Still others possess coefficients which involve a numerical value and one or more units, as was found for G in the law of universal gravitation.

In this regard, it is worth remembering that if the coefficient in a quantity equation involves SI units, say, this does not mean that the other quantities have to be expressed in SI units. As for any quantity equation, the quantities can be expressed in any units we wish. Of course, the units must be appropriate for the quantities.

4.10 Working with *F* = *ma*

The quantity equation $F = ma$ expresses one of the most important natural laws of mechanics. It merits particular attention, for a complete understanding of this equation will eliminate unnecessary confusion.

The equation states clearly that a force F is equal to a mass m times the resulting acceleration a. The following two examples show how easily this equation can accommodate any set of units.

Example 4-1:

A mass of 400 pounds accelerates at a rate of 3 cm/s². Calculate the value of the force.

Solution:

From the quantity equation $F = ma$, (which holds true for any system of units) we have:

$$F = ma$$

$$F = \text{magnitude of mass} \times \text{magnitude of acceleration}$$

$$= 400 \text{ lb} \times 3 \text{ cm/s}^2$$

$$= 1200 \text{ lb} \cdot \text{cm/s}^2$$

The force is, therefore, 1200 pound centimeter per second squared.

Example 4-2:

A mass of 3 kg is acted upon by a force of 6 ozf. Calculate the value of the resulting acceleration.

Solution:

$$\text{From} \quad F = ma$$

$$\text{we have} \quad 6 \text{ ozf} = 3 \text{ kg} \times a$$

$$\text{whence} \quad a = 2 \text{ ozf/kg}$$

The acceleration is therefore 2 ounce force per kilogram.

The answers to these two problems are highly unusual, but they are, nevertheless, correct. Their only shortcoming is that they are expressed in unfamiliar units. We can make these units comprehensible by expressing them in terms of SI base units and by recalling (pages 5, 24) that [newton] = [kg·m/s²]. Let us proceed accordingly.

In Example 4-1, the force is:

$$F = 1200 \text{ lb} \cdot \text{cm/s}^2$$

$$= 1200 \, (\div 2.204 \, 62) \times \text{kg} \times \frac{\text{m}}{100} \times \frac{1}{\text{s}^2}$$

$$= 1200 \times 0.004 \, 535 \, 93 \text{ kg} \cdot \text{m/s}^2$$

$$= 5.443 \text{ newtons} = 5.443 \text{ N}$$

In Example 4-2, the acceleration is:

$$a = 2 \text{ ozf/kg} = 2 \times \text{ozf} \times \frac{1}{\text{kg}}$$

$$= 2 \times \frac{\text{kg·m/s}^2}{3.596\ 94} \times \frac{1}{\text{kg}} \quad \text{(see FORCE chart on page 24)}$$

$$= 0.556 \text{ m/s}^2$$

We can now appreciate the universal nature of the quantity equation $F = ma$, for in the two preceding examples, units from entirely different systems were employed, and yet the correct answer was obtained in every case.

The freedom to use any system of units is the reason why quantity equations are so useful. Their elegant simplicity is also a reflection of the basically simple laws of nature and of the orderly structure of geometry. A list of typical quantity equations appears on pages 84 and 85.

The ensuing examples will further illustrate the versatility of these equations in mechanics, in electricity and in thermodynamics*. We conclude this chapter with a brief overview of the quantities associated with temperature.

4.11 Problems in Geometry and Mechanics

Example 4-3:

Calculate the mass of a sheet of paper 3 feet wide, 4 miles long and 2 millimeters thick if the density is 20 kilograms per cubic foot.

Solution:

To solve this problem, we will first calculate the volume, and then multiply it by the density, as follows:

The quantity equation for volume is $V = lwd$, that is

$$\text{volume} = \text{length} \times \text{width} \times \text{thickness}$$

$$= 4 \text{ mi} \times 3 \text{ ft} \times 2 \text{ mm}$$

$$= 24 \text{ mi·ft·mm}$$

(note that we make no attempt to simplify units at this stage).

The quantity equation for mass is $m = V\rho$, that is:

$$\text{mass} = \text{volume} \times \text{density}$$

$$= 24 \text{ mi·ft·mm} \times 20 \text{ kg/ft}^3$$

$$= 480 \text{ mi·mm·kg/ft}^2$$

and this is the answer to our problem. To make it understandable, we can express

---

* The numerical values given in these problems are assumed to be exact. However, the answers are given to four significant figures.

all units in terms of SI base units. Using the conversion charts, we find:

mass = 480 mi·mm·kg/ft²

$$= 480 \; (\times \; 1.609 \; 344)(\times \; 1000) \; m \times \frac{m}{1000} \times kg \times \frac{1}{(\div \; 9) \; (\div \; 1.195 \; 99) \, m^2}$$

$$= 8315 \; kg$$

There are two advantages in using this "mixed unit" method to solve problems. First, because units are not converted until the end, we are free to deal with the physics of the problem and then look into the question of units. Second, by carrying all units to the end, we have a check on the validity of our calculations. For example, if we had found that the answer to the above problem was, say, 8315 kg/m, we would immediately have known that something was wrong.

Example 4-4:

Calculate the value of the earth's centripetal force which acts on a 150-pound man located at the equator. The radius of the earth is 4000 miles and its angular velocity is 1 revolution per day.

Solution:

The quantity equation for centripetal force is $F = m\omega^2 r$ in which F is the force, m the mass, ω the angular velocity and r the radius.

$$F = m\omega^2 r$$

$$= 150 \; lb \; \times \; [1 \; r/d]^2 \times \; 4000 \; mi$$

$$= 600 \; 000 \; \frac{lb \cdot r^2 \cdot mi}{d^2}$$

Note that the upright letter r stands for the unit [revolution], d stands for [day], while the italic r represents the radius, which is a quantity.

We now convert all units to SI base units. In so doing, we observe from the ANGLE chart (page 10), that the unit [revolution] can *always* be replaced by 2π. We therefore obtain

$$F = 600 \; 000 \times \frac{kg}{2.204 \; 62} \times \frac{[2\pi]^2}{[86 \; 400 \; s]^2} \times 1609.344 \; m$$

$$= 2.316 \; kg \cdot m/s^2 = 2.316 \; N$$

The centripetal force is therefore 2.316 newtons, which is slightly more than half a pound-force.

Example 4-5:

At what speed should a mass of 1 lb move so that its kinetic energy is equal to one electronvolt? Express the answer in centimeters per year.

Solution:

The quantity equation for kinetic energy is:

$$E_k = 1/2 \, mv^2$$

in which m is the mass and v the speed. Let the speed be designated as **S** [cm/a] in which **S** is a pure number and "a" is the symbol for the unit [year]. Using the equation and reducing all units to SI base units, we can write:

$$E_k = \frac{1}{2} mv^2$$

$$1 \text{ eV} = \frac{1}{2} \times 1 \text{ lb} \times \left(\frac{\mathbf{S} \text{ cm}}{a}\right)^2$$

$$\frac{1}{6.241\,51 \times 10^{18}} \frac{\text{kg} \cdot \text{m}^2}{\text{s}^2} = \frac{1}{2} \times \frac{\text{kg}}{2.204\,62} \times \left(\mathbf{S} \times \frac{\text{m}}{100} \times \frac{1}{365 \times 86\,400 \text{ s}}\right)^2$$

$$\frac{1}{6.241\,51 \times 10^{18}} \frac{\text{kg} \cdot \text{m}^2}{\text{s}^2} = \frac{\mathbf{S}^2}{4.385\,07 \times 10^{19}} \frac{\text{kg} \cdot \text{m}^2}{\text{s}^2}$$

all units cancel out and so $\mathbf{S}^2 = 7.025\,66$

$$\text{hence} \quad \mathbf{S} = 2.650$$

The speed is therefore 2.650 cm per year.

4.12 Problems in Electricity

Example 4-6:

A 6-inch conductor sweeps through a magnetic field of 10 kilogauss at a speed of 60 miles per hour. Calculate the value of the induced voltage.

Solution:

The quantity equation for induced voltage is $E = Blv$ in which B is the magnetic flux density, l the length of the conductor and v its speed.

$$E = Blv$$

$$= 10 \text{ kG} \times 6 \text{ in} \times 60 \text{ mi/h}$$

$$= 3600 \text{ kG} \cdot \text{in} \cdot \text{mi/h}$$

The voltage is, therefore, 3600 kilogauss-inch-mile per hour and this is the answer to our problem. We can make the solution more meaningful by expressing all units in terms of SI base units.

$$E = 3600 \times \frac{\text{kg}}{10 \text{ A·s}^2} \times (\times 2.54)(\div100) \text{ m} \times \frac{1609.344 \text{ m}}{3600 \text{ s}}$$

$$= 4.088 \frac{\text{kg·m}^2}{\text{A·s}^3}$$

Noting that $\dfrac{\text{kg·m}^2}{\text{A·s}^3}$ is the expression of the volt in terms of base units (page 17), we find

$$E = 4.088 \text{ V}$$

Example 4-7:
Calculate the resistance of 0.8 miles of copper wire with a cross section of 10 400 circular mils. The resistivity of copper is 1.72 microhm centimeters at 20°C.

Solution:
The quantity equation for the resistance R of a wire is:

$$R = \rho\frac{l}{A}$$

in which ρ is the resistivity, l the length and A the cross section of the wire.

$$R = \rho\frac{l}{A}$$

$$= 1.72 \text{ microhm·cm} \times \frac{0.8 \text{ mi}}{10\ 400 \text{ cmil}}$$

$$= 0.000\ 1323 \frac{\text{ohm·cm}}{10^6} \times \frac{\text{mi}}{\text{cmil}}$$

$$= 1.323 \times 10^{-10} \text{ ohm} \times \frac{\text{m}}{100} \times 1609.344 \text{ m} \times \frac{1}{(\times 506.708)(\div 10^{12})\text{m}^2}$$

$$= 4.202 \text{ ohm} = 4.202 \ \Omega$$

4.13 Problems in Fluids and Heat

Thermodynamics, in common with other sciences, contains a broad spectrum of units drawn from different systems and reflecting different points of view. Slugs, calories, Btu's, degrees Fahrenheit, and so forth, are representative of units that are still widely used, and their diversity is particularly inviting to the quantity equation approach.

Example 4-8:
Calculate the quantity of heat required to raise the temperature of 3 tons of copper from 70 °F to 1000 °F. The specific heat capacity of copper is 0.09 cal/(g·°C).

Solution:

We can use the quantity equation $E = m\theta c$ in which E is the quantity of heat, m the mass of material, θ its temperature rise and c its specific heat. In the absence of specific information regarding the unit [ton] we will assume it is a short ton.

$$E = m\,\theta c$$

$$= 3 \text{ tn} \times (1000 - 70) \text{ °F} \times 0.09 \text{ cal/}(g\cdot°C)$$

$$= 3 \times 930 \times 0.09 \frac{\text{tn}\cdot°F\cdot\text{cal}}{g\cdot°C} = 251.1 \frac{\text{tn}\cdot°F\cdot\text{cal}}{g\cdot°C}$$

expressing all units in terms of SI units, and noting that °F is a temperature *interval* (see TEMPERATURE INTERVAL chart, page 40), we obtain:

$$E = 251.1 \times \frac{2000 \text{ kg}}{2.204\,62} \times \frac{°C}{1.8} \times 4.184 \text{ J} \times \frac{1000}{\text{kg}} \times \frac{1}{°C}$$

$$= 5.295 \times 10^8 \text{ J}$$

The heat required is, therefore,

$$5.295 \times 10^8 \text{ joules} = 529.5 \text{ MJ}$$

or $\qquad 5.295 \times 10^8 (\div 1000) (\div 1.054\,35) \text{ Btu } = 502\,200 \text{ Btu}$

Example 4-9:

The walls of a home are insulated with 8 cm of mineral wool whose thermal conductivity, according to ASHRAE tables, is 0.3 Btu·in/(h·ft^2·°F). If the total surface area of the walls is 150 m^2, calculate the rate of heat loss in Btu per hour when the inside temperature is 20°C and the outside temperature is –15°C.

Solution:

This problem is typical of many problems involving heat flow, in which the published thermal constants may have unusual units. Again, the quantity equation approach makes the calculations simple and unambiguous. Thus, from the quantity equation

$$q = \lambda\theta A/d$$

in which q is the rate of heat flow, λ the thermal conductivity, θ the temperature difference, A the area and d the thickness of the material, we have:

$$q = 0.3 \frac{\text{Btu}\cdot\text{in}}{h\cdot ft^2\cdot°F} \times 150 \text{ m}^2 \times (20-(-15)) \text{ °C} \times \frac{1}{8 \text{ cm}}$$

$$= 196.88 \frac{\text{Btu}\cdot\text{in}\cdot\text{m}^2\cdot°C}{h\cdot ft^2\cdot°F\cdot\text{cm}}$$

We can, of course, express all units in terms of SI base units, but time can often be saved by remembering such ratios as:

$$\frac{in}{cm} = 2.54$$

$$\frac{m}{ft} = \frac{100\,cm}{12\,in} = \frac{100}{12 \times 2.54} = 3.28$$

and for temperature *intervals*

$$\frac{°C}{°F} = 1.8, \quad \text{and so forth.}$$

Using this approach, we find:

$$q = 196.88 \times \frac{Btu}{h} \times \frac{in}{cm} \times \frac{m^2}{ft^2} \times \frac{°C}{°F}$$

$$= 196.88 \frac{Btu}{h} \times 2.54 \times (3.28)^2 \times 1.8$$

$$= 9684.0 \text{ Btu/h}$$

The heat loss is therefore 9684 Btu/h .

or   9684 (÷ 3.414 42) (÷1000) kW = 2.836 kW

Example 4-10:

Five ounces of argon are pumped into a cylinder whose volume is 678 cubic inches. Calculate the pressure in atmospheres if the room temperature is 72 °F. Argon has a molar mass* of 40 g/mol.

Solution:

We will use the quantity equation $pV = nRT$ in which the gas constant R has a value of 8.314 J/(mol·K). The amount of substance n is found from the quantity equation:

$$n = \frac{m}{M}$$

where m is the mass of the substance and M its molecular mass. Thus:

$$n = \frac{m}{M} = \frac{5\,oz}{(40\,g/mol)} = 0.125\,\frac{oz \cdot mol}{g}$$

In the above equation, the symbol T represents the thermodynamic temperature, which means temperature measured from the point of absolute zero (see page 78).

Let the pressure be **X** [atmosphere] in which X is a pure number. Upon substitution, we find:

* Molar mass was occasionally called molecular weight.

$$pV = nRT$$

$$\mathbf{X}\ [\text{atm}] \times 678\ \text{in}^3 = 0.125\ \frac{\text{oz}\cdot\text{mol}}{g} \times 8.314\ \frac{J}{\text{mol}\cdot K} \times 72\ ^\circ F$$

$$\mathbf{X} = 0.001\ 533\ \frac{\text{oz}\cdot J\cdot[72\ ^\circ F]}{g\cdot K\cdot\text{in}^3\cdot\text{atm}}$$

Because $T = 72^\circ F$ is a *Fahrenheit temperature* (see page 80), and not a thermodynamic temperature , the number 72 cannot be treated as a coefficient. We cannot, therefore, multiply 0.001 53 by 72 (as we normally would), but must first convert $72^\circ F$ into its thermodynamic equivalent, expressed in kelvins.

Thus, from the TEMPERATURE conversion chart on page 40, we find :

$72\ ^\circ F = (72 + 459.67)(\div 1.8) = 295.372$ K.

Substituting this value in the above equation, we have

$$\mathbf{X} = 0.001\ 533\ \times 295.372\ \frac{K\cdot\text{oz}\cdot J}{g\cdot K\cdot\text{atm}\cdot\text{in}^3}$$

$$= 0.4528\ \frac{\text{oz}\cdot J}{g\cdot\text{atm}\cdot\text{in}^3}$$

$$= 0.4528 \times 28.3495 \times \frac{J}{\text{atm}\cdot\text{in}^3} = 12.837 \times J \times \frac{1}{\text{atm}} \times \frac{1}{\text{in}^3}$$

$$= 12.837 \times \left(\frac{kg\cdot m^2}{s^2}\right) \times \left(\frac{9.869\ 23\ m\cdot s^2}{1000 \times 1000\ kg}\right) \times \left(\frac{100}{2.54\ m}\right)^3$$

$$\therefore \mathbf{X} = 7.731$$

The units all cancel out (as they should), and the pressure is therefore 7.731 atmospheres.

Example 4-11:

Reynolds number *Re* is an important indicator of fluid turbulence, given by the equation:

$$Re = \frac{v\rho d}{\eta}$$

in which v, ρ and η are respectively the velocity, density and dynamic viscosity of the fluid, and d the diameter of the pipe in which it flows.

Water has a dynamic viscosity of 8×10^{-6} lbf·s/ft^2 at $150^\circ F$ and a density of 1 kilogram per liter. If it flows at 5 miles per hour in a 7/8 inch pipe, calculate *Re* and assess the turbulence. Turbulence occurs when *Re* exceeds roughly 2000.

Solution:

We are dealing with a quantity equation and so any units that are compatible with the quantities can be used. We can therefore substitute the given values as follows:

$$Re = \frac{v\rho d}{\eta}$$

$$= \frac{5\ [\text{mi/h}] \times 1\ [\text{kg/L}] \times 7/8\ [\text{in}]}{8 \times 10^{-6}\ [\text{lbf·s/ft}^2]}$$

$$= 5.469 \times 10^5 \times \frac{\text{mi}}{\text{h}} \times \frac{\text{kg}}{\text{L}} \times \text{in} \times \frac{\text{ft}^2}{\text{lbf·s}}$$

we now convert all units into SI base units and simplify the result:

$$Re = 5.469 \times 10^5 \times \frac{1609.344\ \text{m}}{3600\ \text{s}} \times \frac{\text{kg}}{0.001\ \text{m}^3} \times 2.54\ \text{cm} \times \frac{0.0929\ \text{m}^2}{[4.4482\ \text{N}]\cdot\text{s}}$$

$$= 12.97 \times 10^6 \times \frac{\text{m}}{\text{s}} \times \frac{\text{kg}}{\text{m}^3} \times \frac{\text{m}}{100} \times \frac{\text{m}^2}{\text{N·s}}$$

$$= 1.297 \times 10^5\ \frac{\text{kg·m}}{\text{N·s}^2}$$

recalling that $N = \text{kg·m/s}^2$, the above expression reduces to the dimensionless number $Re = 1.297 \times 10^5$, and since $Re > 2000$, the flow is turbulent.

4.14 Thermodynamic temperature

Temperature, like length and viscosity, is a physical quantity. Indeed, of all the physical quantities, temperature is the one most often measured and quoted. Temperature can range from the very cold, such as that of liquid helium, to the extremely hot, such as that in a nuclear blast.

Temperature is a manifestation of the agitation of atoms and molecules in a body. When this agitation ceases, the temperature is said to be zero. Temperature measured from this level of absolute zero is called the *thermodynamic temperature*. The unit of thermodynamic temperature is the kelvin (symbol K).

The CGPM* defined the kelvin as the fraction 1/273.16 of the thermodynamic temperature of the triple point of water. It follows that the triple point (temperature where water, ice and water vapor coexist in equilibrium) corresponds to a temperature of 273.16 K.

Over the years, several temperature scales were devised, and among these, the Celsius and the Fahrenheit scales are the most familiar.

---

* Conférence générale des poids et mesures (General Conference on Weights and Measures).

4.15 Celsius temperature

By CGPM definition, the physical quantity called *Celsius temperature* (symbol t) is the difference between the thermodynamic temperature T and the thermodynamic temperature of 273.15 K. Thus, the Celsius temperature t is given by the quantity equation:

$$t = T - 273.15 \text{ K} \qquad\qquad (4\text{-}1)$$

It follows that $t = 0$ on the Celsius scale corresponds to $T = 273.15$ K. Celsius temperatures above 273.15 K (the so-called ice point) are positive, while those below are negative. Also by definition, a temperature interval of one degree Celsius is equal to a temperature interval of one degree kelvin, exactly.

Figure 4-1 illustrates graphically the relationship between Celsius temperatures and thermodynamic temperatures.

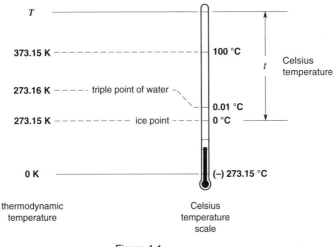

Figure 4-1

We have seen that a temperature interval of one degree Celsius is equal to one kelvin, but in order to avoid confusion, the thermodynamic temperature is always stated in kelvins, while the Celsius temperature is stated in degrees Celsius. However, this does not prevent us from discerningly substituting the units °C for K, and vice versa, in the course of solving a problem.

The conversion from Celsius temperatures to thermodynamic temperatures is readily done by referring to the TEMPERATURE conversion chart on page 40. Contrary to other charts, it involves arrows where arithmetic additions (or subtractions) are required, in addition to the usual multiply/divide arrows.

Example 4-12:

The thermometer of a laboratory oven indicates a temperature of 620 °C. Using the quantity equation (4-1), calculate the thermodynamic temperature of the oven.

Solution:

The thermodynamic temperature T is:

$$T = t + 273.15 \text{ K}$$
$$= 620 \text{ °C} + 273.15 \text{ K}$$
$$= 620 \times \text{°C} + 273.15 \times \text{K}$$

substituting K for °C gives:

$$T = 620 \times \text{K} + 273.15 \times \text{K}$$
$$= 893.15 \text{ K}$$

Note that in making our calculations, we substituted K for °C because these units are identical. Multiplication signs are used above to emphasize the fact that we are dealing with quantities (such as 620 °C).

4.16 Fahrenheit temperature

The Fahrenheit and Centigrade (now called Celsius) temperature scales were both created during the eighteenth century, and the relationship between the two was established at that time. Thus, Figure 4-2 shows that the temperatures 0 °C and 100 °C on the Celsius scale correspond respectively to 32 °F and 212 °F on the Fahrenheit scale.

It follows that a Celsius temperature range of $(100 \text{ °C} - 0 \text{ °C}) = 100 \text{ °C}$ corresponds to a Fahrenheit range of $(212 \text{ °F} - 32 \text{ °F}) = 180 \text{ °F}$. Consequently, the ratio of the unit of Celsius temperature °C to the unit of Fahrenheit temperature °F is given by

$$\frac{\text{°C}}{\text{°F}} = \frac{180}{100} = 1.8$$

Furthermore, knowing that °C = K, we obtain the ratio

$$\frac{\text{K}}{\text{°F}} = 1.8$$

Owing to the linearity of the Fahrenheit and Celsius scales, a temperature of 0 °F corresponds to $-17\frac{7}{9}$ °C $(= -17.\dot{7}$ °C). This, in turn, corresponds to a temperature of $273.15 \text{ K} - 17.\dot{7} \text{ K} = 255.37\dot{2} \text{ K} = 255\frac{67}{180} \text{ K}$ (Figure 4-2).

From this information, and referring again to Figure 4-2, it is clear that the *Fahrenheit temperature* t_F is related to the thermodynamic temperature T by the quantity equation:

$$t_F = T - 255\frac{67}{180} \text{ K}$$

that is, $t_F = T - 255.37\dot{2} \text{ K}$ (4-2)

This quantity equation is similar to quantity equation (4-1) relating the Celsius temperature to the thermodynamic temperature, except that the "reference" temperature is 255.372 K instead of 273.15 K.*

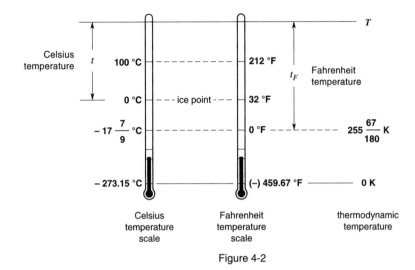

Figure 4-2

Example 4-13:

An outdoor thermometer indicates a temperature of 23 °F. Calculate the thermodynamic temperature T and the temperature that would be shown by a Celsius thermometer. Use the quantity equations (4-1) and (4-2).

Solution:

$$\text{we have} \qquad t_F = T - 255.37\dot{2} \text{ K}$$

$$\text{hence} \qquad 23 \text{ °F} = T - 255.37\dot{2} \text{ K}$$

$$T = 23 \frac{[\text{K}]}{1.8} + 255.37\dot{2} \text{ K}$$

$$= 268.15 \text{ K}$$

Note that in our calculation we replaced the unit °F by its equivalent value K/1.8.

Next, using the quantity equation $t = T - 273.15$ K, we find

$$t = 268.15 \text{ K} - 273.15 \text{ K}$$

$$= -5 \text{ K}$$

$$= -5 \text{ °C}$$

* The reader should refer to Section 5.7, page 96, for temperature conversions based on numerical equations.

Thus, a Celsius thermometer would show $-5\,°C$.

The reader should note that the conversions made here by algebraic means can be made with equal accuracy by using the conversion charts on page 40.

4.17 Temperature interval

Many physical processes involve not temperature as such, but rather temperature differences, also called temperature intervals. Consider two Celsius temperatures t_1 and t_2 defined as usual by $t_1 = T_1 - 273.15\,K$ and $t_2 = T_2 - 273.15\,K$. The difference between the temperatures is

$$t_1 - t_2 = T_1 - T_2$$

This means that the difference in the Celsius temperatures is equal to the difference in the respective *thermodynamic* temperatures. A similar result is obtained using for the quantity equation for the Fahrenheit scale:

$$t_{1F} - t_{2F} = T_1 - T_2$$

Example 4-14:

A Fahrenheit thermometer is used to measure the temperature rise of a hot-water tank. The temperature increases from 60 °F to 87 °F in two hours. Express the temperature rise in kelvins and in degrees Celsius.

Solution:

The temperatue rise is $(87\,°F - 60\,°F) = 27\,°F$. Since $K = 1.8\,°F$, the temperature rise in kelvins is

$$27\,°F \;=\; 27\,°F \times \frac{K}{K} \;=\; 27 \times \frac{°F}{K} \times K \;=\; 27 \times \frac{1}{1.8} \times K \;=\; 15\,K$$

Also, because $K = °C$, the temperature interval is equal to $15\,°C$.

REVIEW QUESTIONS

Using the quantity equations on pages 84-85, calculate the following

4.1   The area (in square centimeters) of a rectangle 4 feet wide and 2 inches long.

4.2   The volume (in cubic centimeters) of a box that is 4 feet wide, 2 yards long and 3 cm high.

4.3   The mass (in kilograms) of a body whose density is 8 g/cm^3 and whose volume is 2 ft^3.

4.4   The momentum (in newton seconds) of a bullet whose mass is 3 oz, moving at 600 mi/h (use equation 16).

4.5. The work done (in joules) by a force of 10 newtons when it moves 10 feet.

4.6   The power (in watts) produced by an engine which revolves at 1000 r/min and develops a torque of 5 N·m (use equation 25).

4.7   The amount of substance (in moles) contained in a mass of 414 lb of lead whose atomic weight is 207 g/mol (use equation 36).

4.8 The amount of heat (in Btu) added to 2 kg of copper when its temperature is raised by 10 °F. The specific heat is 0.09 cal/g·°C. (use equation 38)

4.9 The peripheral velocity (in meters per second) of a body which revolves at 200 r/min 4 feet from the centre of rotation. (use equation 9)

4.10 The distance (in miles) covered by a body in 3 h if it moves at 6 m/min.

4.11 Calculate the mass (in kilograms) of a sheet of material 4 meters wide, 8 feet long and 1/10 inch thick, knowing that its density is 8 grams per cubic centimeter. (use equation 13)

4.12 A metallic sphere 40 cm in diameter has a density of 480 lb/ft^3. Calculate its mass in kilograms. (use equations 4 and 13)

4.13. A revolving stone at the end of a string is moving at 150 miles per hour. If the string is 2 meters long, how fast is the stone revolving in revolutions per minute? (use equation 9)

4.14 A body initially moving at 40 mi/h, accelerates at 0.1 m/s^2 for a period of 2 minutes. What is the final speed in m/s? (use equation 5)

4.15 A mass of 5 lb is suspended from the end of a 15 in arm. The local value of $g = 9.807$ m/s^2. Calculate the torque in N·m. (use equations 18, 19)

4.16 A motor running at 1800 r/min develops a torque of 9 lbf·ft. What is its horsepower? (use equation 25)

4.17 A 2 oz mass possesses a kinetic energy of 10 joules. How fast is it moving in ft/s? (use equation 24)

4.18 A mass of 6 lb is transported to the moon where its weight is found to be only 1 lbf. Calculate the acceleration (in m/s^2) if the mass is allowed to fall.

4.19 A steel cylinder 11 in in diameter and 2 ft long, revolves around its axis at a speed of 200 r/min. Calculate its kinetic energy (in joules) knowing that steel has a density of 8 kg/dm^3. (use equations 2, 13, 17 and 27)

4.20 Water flows from a pipe at the rate of 1000 gal (CAN)/min . How many hours will it take to fill a 2 acre pond to a depth of 1 meter?

4.21 A mass of 10 slugs turns at 60 revolution/min at the end of a 2 meter rod. Calculate its kinetic energy (in joules) and the tension in the rod in newtons. (use equations 9, 24, 26)

4.22 Calculate the kinetic energy (in megajoules) of a 4000 lb car moving at 70 mi/h. (use equation 24)

4.23 Calculate the approximate mass of the carth (in yottagrams), knowing (a) that the force of gravity is about 150 lbf on a man who has a mass of 150 lb and (b) that the radius of the earth is 4000 miles. (use equation 29)

4.24 A blackbody has an area of 4 square feet and it radiates 10 Btu/s. What is its temperature (a) in kelvins, (b) in °C ? (use equation 37)

4.25 A column of mercury 20 in high and having a density of 13.6 g/cm^3 is located in a lab where the acceleration of free fall is 32 ft/s^2. Calculate the pressure (in kilopascals) exerted at the base of the column. (use equation 32)

TYPICAL QUANTITY EQUATIONS

Geometry

1	$A = lw$	area A of rectangle, length l, width w
2	$A = \pi r^2$	area A of circle, radius r
3	$A = 4\pi r^2$	surface area A of sphere, radius r
4	$V = \dfrac{4}{3}\pi r^3$	volume V of sphere, radius r

Space and time

5	$v = v_0 + at$	Equations 5, 6, 7:
6	$s = v_0 t + 1/2\, at^2$	initial velocity v_0, final velocity v,
7	$v^2 = v_0^2 + 2as$	acceleration a, time t, distance s
8	$\omega = d\theta/dt$	angular velocity ω, angle θ, time t
9	$v = \omega r$	peripheral velocity v, angular velocity ω, radius r
10	$\omega = 2\pi f$	angular velocity ω, frequency f
11	$T = 2\pi/\omega = 1/f$	period T of one cycle, angular velocity ω, frequency f
12	$a = \omega^2 r$	acceleration a, angular velocity ω, radius r

Mechanics

13	$\rho = m/V$	density ρ, mass m, volume V
14	$p = F/A$	pressure p, force F, area A
15	$W = Fs$	work W, force F, displacement s
16	$p = mv$	momentum p, mass m, velocity v
17	$J = 1/2\, mr^2$	moment of inertia J of a cylinder, mass m, radius r
18	$W = mg$	weight W of a mass m, acceleration of free fall g
19	$T = Fr$	torque T, force F, radius arm r
20	$E = \sigma/\varepsilon$	Young's modulus E, stress σ, strain ε
21	$\sigma = F/A$	stress σ, force F, area A
22	$\varepsilon = \Delta l/l$	strain ε, elongation Δl, initial length l
23	$E_p = mgh$	potential energy E_p, mass m, acceleration of free fall g, height h
24	$E_k = 1/2\, mv^2$	kinetic energy E_k, mass m, velocity v
25	$P = \omega T$	power P, angular velocity ω, torque T
26	$F = m\omega^2 r$	centripetal force F, mass m, angular velocity ω, radius r
27	$E_k = 1/2\, J\omega^2$	kinetic energy E_k, moment of inertia J, angular velocity ω
28	$F = ma$	force F, mass m, acceleration a
29	$F = G\dfrac{m_1 m_2}{d^2}$	force of gravity F, masses m_1, m_2, distance d, $G \approx 6.673 \times 10^{-11}\,\text{N·m}^2\,\text{kg}^{-2}$
30	$F = ks$	force F, spring constant k, elongation s

31 $\quad f = \dfrac{1}{2\pi} \sqrt{\dfrac{k}{m}}$ frequency f, mass m, spring constant k, (mass/spring system)

Fluids and gases

32 $\quad p = \rho g h$ pressure p, density ρ, acceleration of free fall g, of a column of fluid having a height h

33 $\quad v = \sqrt{2gh}$ velocity of fluid discharge v, height h, acceleration free fall g

34 $\quad pV = nRT$ pressure p, volume V, amount of substance n, gas constant R, temperature T ($R = 8.314\,34$ J/(mol·K))

35 $\quad n = N/N_A$ amount of substance n, number of entities N, Avogadro's number N_A ($N_A = 6.022 \times 10^{23}$ per mol); N is a pure number

36 $\quad n = m/M$ amount of substance n, mass m, molecular or atomic mass M

Heat

37 $\quad P = \sigma A T^4$ radiation power P of a black body, area A, temperature T ($\sigma = 5.6705 \times 10^{-8}$ W/(m²·K⁴))

38 $\quad E = mc\theta$ heat energy E, mass m, temperature rise θ, specific heat c

39 $\quad t = T - 273.15$ K Celsius temperature t, thermodynamic temperature T

40 $\quad t_F = t + 17\tfrac{7}{9}$ K Fahrenheit temperature t_F, Celsius temperature t (as quantities)

Electricity and magnetism

41 $\quad F = \dfrac{Q_1 Q_2}{4 \pi \varepsilon_0 \varepsilon_r d^2}$ force F between point charges Q_1, Q_2, distance d,

permittivity ε_0, relative permittivity ε_r ($\varepsilon_0 = 8.854 \times 10^{-12}$ F/m, ε_r is a pure number)

42 $\quad R = \rho l/A$ resistance R, resistivity ρ, length l, cross section A

43 $\quad F = Bli$ force F on a conductor of length l carrying a current i, at right angles to magnetic flux density B

44 $\quad E = Blv$ voltage E induced in a conductor of length l, moving at speed v, at right angles to magnetic flux density B

45 $\quad f = \dfrac{1}{2\pi} \sqrt{\dfrac{1}{LC}}$ resonance frequency f, inductance L, capacitance C

46 $\quad E = N \dfrac{d\Phi}{dt}$ voltage E induced in a coil of N turns, flux Φ, time t

Waves and sound

47 $\quad v = \sqrt{E/\rho}$ velocity v of sound in a long rod of density ρ, Young's modulus E

48 $\quad \lambda = v/f$ wavelength λ, velocity v, frequency f

5

NUMERICAL EQUATIONS

We have seen that quantity equations give the relationship between physical quantities, and such equations can be used with any system of units. Sometimes, however, it is convenient to set up an equation to accommodate a particular group of units. Such an equation is called a *numerical* equation because all its terms represent pure numbers. Numerical equations are also called *measure* equations.

We can readily transform a quantity equation into a numerical equation by specifying the units we wish to employ.

Many difficulties involving units arise from a failure to distinguish between quantity equations and numerical equations. It must be assumed that whenever the units of an equation are specified, we are dealing with a numerical equation, whose terms represent pure numbers.

The following equation, drawn from an engineering handbook, is a typical example of a numerical equation. It gives the power output of a wind-driven electric generator as a function of the diameter of a 2-blade windmill and the speed of the wind:

$$\mathbf{P} = 1.19 \times 10^{-3} \, \mathbf{D}^2 \mathbf{V}^3$$

in which

$\mathbf{P}$ = power output of the generator, in watts
$\mathbf{D}$ = diameter of the windmill, in feet
$\mathbf{V}$ = speed of the wind, in miles per hour

Note that the units (watt, foot, mile/hour) for $\mathbf{P}$, $\mathbf{D}$ and $\mathbf{V}$ are specified, which indicates that this is indeed a numerical equation.

Although there is no precedent to do so, we will use capitalized bold upright letters to designate the symbols used in numerical equations. This is to clearly distinguish them from the italic letter symbols used in quantity equations.

Example 5-1:

Calculate the power generated by a 2-blade, 8-foot windmill when the wind is blowing at 20 miles per hour.

Solution:

The power is:

$$\mathbf{P} = 1.19 \times 10^{-3}\ \mathbf{D^2V^3}$$

$$\mathbf{P} = 1.19 \times 10^{-3} \times 8^2 \times 20^3$$

$$= 609$$

The power is therefore 609 W. This example shows that numerical equations can be solved by simply plugging in numbers - and therein lies their principal advantage. Contrary to quantity equations, we don't have to bother with carrying along units.

5.1 Creating a numerical equation

A simple example involving area will show how a numerical equation is created. In effect, we begin with a quantity equation and transform it into a numerical equation. The quantity equation for the area of a rectangle is given by

$$A = lw$$

where l is the length and w is the width. It can be used with any units, but suppose we often had to work with the length in miles, the width in yards and the area in acres. It would then be convenient to employ only the *number* of [miles], the *number* of [yards] and the *number* of [acres] to determine the length, width or area of the rectangle.

Therefore, let $\mathbf{A}$ be the number of acres, $\mathbf{L}$ the number of miles and $\mathbf{W}$ the number of yards. Because a quantity is always equal to the product of a number times a unit, we can write:

$$A = lw \qquad \text{(the quantity equation)}$$

$$\{\text{number of acres}\}[\text{acre}] = \{\text{number of miles}\}[\text{mile}] \times \{\text{number of yards}\}[\text{yard}]$$

$$\mathbf{A}\ [\text{acre}] = \mathbf{L}\ [\text{mi}] \times \mathbf{W}\ [\text{yd}]$$

$$\mathbf{A} = \mathbf{LW} \times \frac{[\text{mi}] \cdot [\text{yd}]}{[\text{acre}]}$$

Using the charts (pages 12 and 25) to reduce all units to SI base units, we find:

$$\mathbf{A} = \mathbf{LW} \times \frac{1609.344\ [\text{m}] \times \dfrac{[\text{m}]}{1.093\ 61}}{(\times 43\ 560)(\div 9)(\div 1.195\ 99)[\text{m}^2]}$$

$$= \mathbf{LW} \times 0.364$$

hence $\mathbf{A} = 0.364\ \mathbf{LW}$

All units cancel out and we are left with a coefficient (0.364) that is a pure number.

This is a numerical equation in which the symbols **A**, **L** and **W** represent pure numbers, respectively equal to the number of acres, the number miles and the number of yards.

It is obvious that we could generate many more numerical equations using the quantity equation $A = lw$, depending upon the units of width, length and area we want to use.

5.2 Transforming a quantity equation into a numerical equation

The preceding example shows that to transform a quantity equation into a numerical equation, we adopt the following procedure:

1. Select the appropriate quantity equation,

2. For each physical quantity Q_x in the quantity equation, assign the unit $[U_x]$ desired for that quantity,

3. For each physical quantity Q_x, assign a symbol $\{N_x\}$ to represent the number of units in that quantity,

4. Replace each quantity Q_x by the product $\{N_x\}\,[U_x]$

5. Express each unit $[U_x]$ in terms of SI base units, and check that the resulting group of base units cancel out to yield a coefficient that is a pure number.

The following examples illustrate the generality of the method to convert quantity equations into numerical equations.

Example 5-2:

Transform the quantity equation distance = speed × time into a numerical equation with the distance in [statute miles], the speed in [knots] and the time in [hours].

Solution:

We adopt the following procedure:

1. Select the appropriate quantity equation,

$$s = vt$$

2. For each quantity Q_x in the quantity equation, assign the desired unit $[U_x]$, and a symbol N_x to represent the number of units. Thus:

since $Q_x = N_x\,[U_x]$

we can write   distance $s = S$ [mi]

speed $v = V$ [knot]

time $t = T$ [h]

in which **S**, **V** and **T** are pure numbers. If we substitute the above in the quantity equation $s = vt$ we obtain:

$$s = vt$$

$$\text{S [mi]} = \text{V [knot]} \times \text{T [h]}$$

$$\text{S} = \text{VT} \frac{\text{[knot]·[h]}}{\text{[mi]}}$$

reducing all units to SI base units yields:

$$\text{S} = \text{VT} \times \frac{\frac{\text{[m/s]}}{1.944} \times 3600 \text{ [s]}}{1609.344 \text{ [m]}}$$

$$= \text{VT} \times 1.15$$

and so $\quad$ $\text{S} = 1.15 \text{ VT}$

We note that all units cancel out, yielding the coefficient 1.15, and the numerical equation **S** = 1.15 **VT**, where **S** is the *number* of miles, **V** is the *number* of knots, and **T** is the *number* of hours.

Example 5-3:

The heat energy required to raise the temperature of a mass *m* of material through a temperature range θ is given by the quantity equation:

$$E = mc\,\theta$$

where

E = heat energy
m = mass of material
c = specific heat
θ = temperature rise

Determine the numerical equation when E is expressed in Btu, m in pounds, c in cal/(kg·°C) and θ in °F.

Solution:

Replacing each quantity by the desired unit plus a letter symbol representing the corresponding number of units, we obtain the following result:

$$Q = mc\,\theta$$

$$\text{E [Btu]} = \text{M [lb]} \times \text{C} \frac{\text{[cal]}}{\text{[kg.°C]}} \times \Theta \text{ [°F]}$$

$$\text{E} = \text{MC}\Theta \times \frac{\text{[cal]}}{\text{[Btu]}} \times \frac{\text{[lb]}}{\text{[kg]}} \times \frac{\text{[°F]}}{\text{[°C]}}$$

$$\text{E} = \text{MC}\Theta \times \frac{1}{251.996} \times \frac{1}{2.204\,62} \times \frac{1}{1.8}$$

whence $\quad$ $\text{E} = 0.001 \text{ MC}\Theta$

The numerical equation is therefore **E** = 0.001 **MCΘ**.

The preceding examples again show that every term of a numerical equation represents a *number* of units.

It is obvious that a numerical equation is useless if we do not know the units that are associated with each term. A quantity equation imposes no such restriction, for as long as we know the physical quantity that each term represents, the equation can be solved. However, numerical equations are very handy because they do not require units to be carried along with our calculations.

5.4 Transforming a numerical equation into a quantity equation

We have seen that many formulas given in handbooks and elsewhere are numerical equations tied to a particular set of units. We can transform such equations into quantity equations and thereby render them universal. Such transformations are simply the reverse of converting quantity equations into numerical equations, a procedure we have just covered. In effect, the transformation is based upon the simple rule that:

$$\text{quantity} = \{\text{number of units}\} \times [\text{unit}]$$

$$Q_x = N_x [U_x]$$

$$\text{that is} \quad N_x = \frac{Q_x}{[U_x]}$$

Because a numerical equation involves symbols that represent the number N_x of units, we can convert it into a quantity equation by substituting these N_x symbols, term by term, with the value $Q_x / [U_x]$ where $[U_x]$ is the unit specified in the numerical equation.

To illustrate the method, let us transform the numerical equation given at the beginning of this chapter

$$P = 1.19 \times 10^{-3} \, D^2 V^3$$

into a quantity equation. We recall that in this equation

P = power output of the generator, in watts
D = diameter of the windmill, in feet
V = speed of the wind, in miles/hour

Let us use the quantity symbols p, d, v to represent the power, diameter, and speed. We then replace the numerical symbols P, D, V, term by term, by the corresponding ratios $Q_x / [U_x]$, as shown below:

$$P = 1.19 \times 10^{-3} \, D^2 V^3$$

$$\frac{p}{[\text{watt}]} = 1.19 \times 10^{-3} \left(\frac{d}{[\text{foot}]}\right)^2 \left(\frac{v}{[\text{mile/hour}]}\right)^3$$

$$\frac{p}{[\text{W}]} = 1.19 \times 10^{-3} \left(\frac{d}{[\text{ft}]}\right)^2 \left(\frac{v}{[\text{mi/h}]}\right)^3$$

whence $p = 1.19 \times 10^{-3} \, d^2 \, v^3 \, [\text{W}] \left(\frac{1}{[\text{ft}]}\right)^2 \left(\frac{1}{[\text{mi/h}]}\right)^3$

thus $p = 1.19 \times 10^{-3} \, d^2 \, v^3 \, [\text{W}] \left(\frac{1}{[\text{ft}]}\right)^2 \left(\frac{[\text{h}]}{[\text{mi}]}\right)^3$

Expressing all units in terms of SI base units, we find

$$p = 1.19 \times 10^{-3} \, d^2 v^3 \left[\frac{\text{kg}\cdot\text{m}^2}{\text{s}^3}\right] \left(\frac{3 \times 1.093\ 61}{[\text{m}]}\right)^2 \left(\frac{3600\ [\text{s}]}{1609.344\ [\text{m}]}\right)^3$$

$$= 0.143 \, d^2 v^3 \left[\frac{\text{kg}\cdot\text{m}^2}{\text{s}^3}\right] \left(\frac{1}{[\text{m}]}\right)^2 \left(\frac{[\text{s}]}{[\text{m}]}\right)^3$$

$$= 0.143 \, \frac{[\text{kg}]}{[\text{m}]^3} \, d^2 v^3$$

yielding the quantity equation

$$p = k_\text{w} \, d^2 v^3 \qquad \text{in which } k_\text{w} = 0.143 \text{ kg/m}^3$$

This quantity equation has a coefficient $k_\text{w} = 0.143$ kg/m³, in addition to the symbols d and v for the diameter of the windmill and the speed of the wind.

Example 5-4:

The following equation, described in a textbook, gives the relationship between the pressure, volume, mass and temperature of dry air:

$$\textbf{PV} = 53.34 \, \textbf{MT}$$

in which

    P = pressure, in lbf/ft²
    V = volume, in ft³
    M = mass, in lb
    T = temperature, in degrees Rankine

Transform this equation into a quantity equation.

Solution:

Because units are specified in this equation, we can be sure that all its terms represent pure numbers. We can convert it into a quantity equation involving the physical quantities p, v, m and T by observing that the *number* of units is equal to the quantity divided by the unit.

Again using this technique, and substituting in the equation

$$\mathbf{PV} = 53.34 \ \mathbf{MT}$$

we find

$$\frac{p}{[\text{lbf/ft}^2]} \times \frac{V}{[\text{ft}^3]} = 53.34 \ \frac{m}{[\text{lb}]} \times \frac{T}{[°\text{R}]}$$

$$pV = 53.34 \ \frac{\text{lbf·ft}}{\text{lb·°R}} \ mT \qquad (R_{\text{air}} \text{ form 1})$$

whence $\quad pV = R_{\text{air}} \ mT$

in which $\quad R_{\text{air}} = 53.34 \ \dfrac{\text{lbf·ft}}{\text{lb·°R}}$

This is the desired quantity equation. The coefficient $R_{\text{air}} = 53.34 \ \text{lbf·ft/(lb·°R)}$ can be converted to SI base units, but this conversion is not essential; the equation is complete as it stands.

If we *do* convert R_{air} to SI base units, the quantity equation becomes:

$$pV = 53.34 \ \frac{[\text{lbf}]\cdot[\text{ft}]}{[\text{lb}]\cdot[°\text{R}]} \ mT$$

$$= 53.34 \times \frac{[4.448 \ 22 \times \text{kg·m/s}^2] \times \dfrac{[\text{m}]}{3 \times 1.093 \ 61}}{\dfrac{[\text{kg}]}{2.204 \ 62} \times \dfrac{[\text{K}]}{1.8}} \ mT$$

i.e. $\quad pV = 287 \ \dfrac{\text{m}^2}{\text{K·s}^2} \ mT \qquad (R_{\text{air}} \text{ form 2})$

which can also be expressed as

$$pV = 287 \ \frac{\text{J}}{\text{kg·K}} \ mT \qquad (R_{\text{air}} \text{ form 3})$$

In the physical equation $pV = R_{\text{air}} mT$, the coefficient R_{air} can be expressed in three different ways, all of which amount to the same quantity. The expression we use is arbitrary, but in the interest of coherence*, preference is given to the SI form, namely:

$$R_{\text{air}} = 287 \ \frac{\text{J}}{\text{kg·K}} \quad \text{or} \quad R_{\text{air}} = 287 \ \frac{\text{m}^2}{\text{K·s}^2} \quad \text{rather than} \quad R_{\text{air}} = 53.34 \ \frac{\text{lbf·ft}}{\text{lb·°R}}$$

* See Section 5.6

Example 5-5:

During an experiment, the following relationship was found to exist between the fusing current of a copper conductor and its diameter.

$$I = 70\ \mathbf{D}^{1.5}$$

in which

   I = current, in amperes
   D = diameter, in millimeters

Develop a physical equation to describe this relationship.

Solution:

This numerical equation is typical of many empirical equations in which the relationships are determined experimentally.

Referring to the equation, we substitute the numerical values I and D by the respective quantities I and d divided by the corresponding units. Thus,

$$I = 70\ \mathbf{D}^{1.5}$$

$$\frac{I}{[A]} = 70\ \left(\frac{d}{[mm]}\right)^{1.5}$$

$$I = d^{1.5}\ 70\ [A]\ [mm]^{-1.5}$$

$$= d^{1.5}\ 70\ [A]\ \left[\frac{m}{1000}\right]^{-1.5}$$

$$= d^{1.5}\ 70\ [A]\ [m]^{-1.5}\ [1000]^{1.5}$$

$$= 2.21\ \times\ 10^6\ [A]\ [m]^{-1.5}\ d^{1.5}$$

Thus, we obtain the quantity equation

   $I = k\ d^{1.5}$

in which

   I = fusing current
   d = diameter of the conductor
   k = physical constant whose value is 2.21×10^6 A·m$^{-1.5}$

This example also shows that units can be treated like algebraic symbols, even when fractional exponents are involved.

5.5 Transforming numerical equations

Suppose a given numerical equation employs units that do not correspond to the units of the quantities we have. In such cases, we can transform the numerical equation into a quantity equation and simply introduce the quantities. However, we may prefer to transform the given numerical equation into a new numerical equation whose symbols represent the desired units.

For example, suppose that in a given numerical equation a particular term N_A is associated with a [unit A]. We want to replace this numerical term by a new term N_B, associatedwith [unit B]. We reason as follows.

The magnitude Q of a quantity must remain the same whether expressed in terms of [unit A] or [unit B]. Thus, we can write

$$Q = \{N_A\} \,[\text{unit A}] = \{N_B\} \,[\text{unit B}]$$

which gives
$$\{N_A\} = \{N_B\} \frac{[\text{unit B}]}{[\text{unit A}]}$$

Thus, to make the transformation, we simply replace the original term N_A by the expression $N_B \dfrac{[\text{unit B}]}{[\text{unit A}]}$. The ratio [unit B]/[unit A] will automatically reduce to a pure number, which is integrated into the new numerical equation.

Example 5-6:

In Example 5-5, the numerical equation relating the fusing current to the diameter of a copper wire is given by

$$I = 70 \, D^{1.5}$$

in which I = current, in amperes and D = diameter, in millimeters.

Determine the numerical equation when the current is expressed in kiloamperes and the diameter in inches.

Solution:

Let $\{I_B\}$ represent the current in kA, and $\{D_B\}$ the diameter in inches. We can therefore make the following substitutions:

I can be replaced by $\{I_B\} \dfrac{[\text{kA}]}{[\text{A}]}$, which reduces to $1000 \,\{I_B\}$

and D can be replaced by $\{D_B\} \dfrac{[\text{inch}]}{[\text{mm}]}$, which reduces to $25.4 \,\{D_B\}$

since $I = 70 \, D^{1.5}$

by substitution we obtain $1000 \,\{I_B\} = 70 \,(25.4 \,\{D_B\})^{1.5}$

The new numerical equation is therefore $\mathbf{I_B} = 8.96\ \mathbf{D_B}^{1.5}$

in which $\mathbf{I_B}$ = current, in kA and $\mathbf{D_B}$ = diameter, in inches

5.6 Meaning of coherence

A system of units is said to be *coherent* when the numerical equations, expressed in this system of units, have the same form as the corresponding quantity equations. Coherence is one of the distinguishing features of the SI. The following list of equations illustrates the meaning of coherence. The similarity between the

Quantity Equation	Numerical Equation
$W = Fd$	$\mathbf{W} = \mathbf{Fd}$
$d = 1/2\ at^2$	$\mathbf{d} = 1/2\ \mathbf{at^2}$
$F = ma$	$\mathbf{F} = \mathbf{ma}$
$E = 1/2\ mv^2$	$\mathbf{E} = 1/2\ \mathbf{mv^2}$
$F = G\,m_1 m_2 / d^2$	$\mathbf{F} = \mathbf{G\,m_1 m_2 / d^2}$
$F = m\omega^2 r$	$\mathbf{F} = \mathbf{m\omega^2 r}$

in which
W = work
F = force
d = distance
E = energy
m = mass
v = velocity
a = acceleration
ω = angular velocity
t = time
$G = 6.673 \times 10^{-11}\ \mathrm{m^3 \cdot kg^{-1} \cdot s^{-2}}$

in which
$\mathbf{W}$ = work, in joules
$\mathbf{F}$ = force, in newtons
$\mathbf{d}$ = distance, in meters
$\mathbf{E}$ = energy, in joules
$\mathbf{m}$ = mass, in kilograms
$\mathbf{v}$ = velocity, in m/s
$\mathbf{a}$ = acceleration, in m/s^2
ω = angular velocity, in rad/s
$\mathbf{t}$ = time, in seconds
$\mathbf{G} = 6.673 \times 10^{-11}$

Note that the coefficient G is composed of a numerical factor and SI base units.

Note that the numerical factor $\mathbf{G} = 6.673 \times 10^{-11}$ is the same as that of G in the quantity equation.

The symbols represent quantities. They are always shown in italics.

The symbols represent numbers, here shown in bold roman characters.

quantity equations and the numerical equations is obvious when SI units are used. Note that when quantity equations involve coefficients that contain units (such as G above), they must also be expressed in SI units, in order to maintain coherence.

This means that any quantity equation in which the coefficient is expressed in SI base units and a number, can immediately be transformed into a numerical equation. In solving the numerical equation, it is important that all numerical values be related to SI base and derived units, but not their multiples or submultiples. In this regard, we recall that the kilogram is a base unit, despite the fact that it bears the prefix "kilo".

Example 5-7:

The quantity equation in Example 5-5 was found to be

$$I = 2.21 \times 10^6 \text{ A·m}^{-1.5} d^{1.5}$$

Determine the fusing current for a wire having a diameter of 2 mm.

Solution:

When SI units are used, the numerical equation can be written down by inspection. We retain only the numerical part of the coefficient, dropping the SI component A·m$^{-1.5}$. This yields the result:

$$\mathbf{I} = 2.21 \times 10^6 \mathbf{d}^{1.5}$$

substituting $\mathbf{d} = 0.002$, we obtain: $\mathbf{I} = 2.21 \times 10^6 (0.002)^{1.5} = 197.7$

The fusing current is therefore 197.7 amperes.

It is clear that the coherent nature of SI permits us to move easily from quantity equations to SI-based numerical equations.

5.7 Transforming temperature equations into numerical equations

We recall that two temperature equations (4-1) and (4-2) were given on pages 79 and 80:

$$t = T - 273.15 \text{ K} \qquad \text{Eq. (4-1)}$$

$$t_F = T - 255.372 \text{ K} \qquad \text{Eq. (4-2)}$$

These are the basic *quantity* equations relating the thermodynamic temperature to Celsius and Fahrenheit temperatures, respectively. However, these equations are usually presented in the form of numerical equations. Owing to the coherence of the SI, the numerical equation corresponding to equation (4-1) has the same form as the quantity equation. Again using bold roman typeface for numerical values, we can immediately write the numerical equation:

$$\mathbf{t} = \mathbf{T} - 273.15$$

in which **t** is the temperature in degrees Celsius, **T** is the thermodynamic temperature in kelvins, and 273.15 is a pure number.

As regards quantity equation (4-2), the numerical equation is deduced in the usual manner. Thus, expressing the respective quantities t_F and T as the product of a number times the desired unit gives:

$$\mathbf{t}_F \text{ [°F]} = \mathbf{T} \text{ [K]} - 255.372 \text{ K}$$

in which $\mathbf{t}_F$ is the *number* of degrees Fahrenheit and **T** is the *number* of kelvins. Transposing [°F], and recalling that [K]/[°F] = 1.8, we obtain:

$$t_F = T \ \frac{[K]}{[°F]} - 255.37 \ \dot{2} \ \frac{[K]}{[°F]}$$

$$= 1.8 \ T - 255.37 \ \dot{2} \times 1.8$$

Consequently,

$$t_F = 1.8 \ T - 459.67$$

is the numerical equation relating thermodynamic and Fahrenheit temperatures.

REVIEW QUESTIONS

See pages 84-85 for equations referred to in the problems.

Convert the following quantity equations into numerical equations:

5.1   From the quantity equation $F = ma$ deduce the numerical equation with

    F in [poundal]   **M** in [lb]   **A** in $[ft/s^2]$

5.2   From the quantity equation $F = ma$ deduce the numerical equation with

    F in [lbf]   **M** in [slug]   **A** in $[ft/s^2]$

5.3   From the quantity equation (25) $P = \omega T$, deduce the numerical equation with **P** in horsepower, **W** in r/min, and **T** in ft·lbf.

5.4   From the quantity equation (42) $F = BlI$, deduce the numerical equation with **F** in lbf, **B**in lines per square inch, **L** in feet, **I** in amperes.

5.5   From the quantity equation (26) $F = m\omega^2 r$, deduce the numerical equation with **F** in lbf, **M** in lb, **W** in r/min, **R** in ft.

5.6   From the quantity equation $B = \mu_0 H$, where B is the flux density, H the magnetic field strength and $\mu_0 = 4\pi \times 10^{-7}$ henrys per meter, deduce the numerical equation with **B** in gauss and **H** in oersted.

5.7   From the quantity equation (34) $pV = nRT$, deduce the numerical equation with **P** in pound force per square inch, **V** in cubic feet, **n** in moles and T_F in °F.

Convert the following numerical equations to quantity equations:

5.8   The area of a field is given by the equation $A = 0.000 \ 247 \ \mathbf{xy}$

    in which **A** is the area in acres, and **x, y** are the length of the sides in meters. Use symbols A, l, w for the quantities area, length and width.

5.9   The peripheral speed of a revolving body is given by the equation:

$$V = 4.282 \ \mathbf{WR}$$

    in which **V** is the speed in mi/h, **W** is the speed of rotation in revolutions per second and **R** is the radius in feet. Determine the quantity equation in which v, ω and r are the speed, rate of rotation and radius, respectively.

5.10 The force of attraction between two point charges is given by the equation

$$\mathbf{F} = \frac{\mathbf{Q_1 Q_2}}{\mathbf{D}^2}$$

in which $\mathbf{F}$ is the force in dynes, $\mathbf{Q_1}$ and $\mathbf{Q_2}$ is the charge in statcoulombs and $\mathbf{D}$ is the distance between them, in centimeters. Find the quantity equation in which F, Q_1, Q_2 and d are the force, charge and distance respectively (express the coefficient of the quantity equation in SI base units).

5.11 The force of attraction of a magnet upon a piece of steel is given by the equation

$$\mathbf{F} = \frac{\mathbf{B}^2\mathbf{A}}{72 \times 10^6}$$

In which $\mathbf{F}$ is the force in lbf, $\mathbf{B}$ is the density in maxwells/in^2 and $\mathbf{A}$ is the area of the poles in in^2. Find the quantity equation in which F, B and A are the force, flux density and area respectively (express the coefficient in SI base units).

5.12 The discharge of air from an orifice is given by the equation

$$\mathbf{W} = 0.0137\ \mathbf{D}^2 \sqrt{\frac{\mathbf{I}\,\mathbf{P}}{\mathbf{F} + 459.67}}$$

in which
    $\mathbf{W}$ = rate of mass discharged, in pounds per second
    $\mathbf{D}$ = diameter of orifice, in inches
    $\mathbf{I}$ = difference of pressure, in inches of water
    $\mathbf{P}$ = mean absolute pressure, in pound-force per square foot
    $\mathbf{F}$ = temperature, in °F

Convert this formula into a quantity equation using the corresponding quantity symbols w, d, I, P, T, where T is the thermodynamic temperature. Express the coefficient in SI units.

6

MASS, FORCE, AND GRAVITY

We have seen that the SI unit of force, the newton, is defined as that force which will impart to a mass of 1 kg an acceleration of 1 m/s^2.

We could also have defined the newton as that force which will stretch a standardized steel spring by a distance of 1 cm. The apparent simplicity of this method of defining the unit of force conceals a number of important practical difficulties. The length and uniform cross section of the spring, the quality of the steel, aging, and temperature are only a few of the factors that would have to be accurately controlled. It is doubtful whether the newton, standardized and measured this way would be accurate to more than one part in ten thousand. Surprising as it may seem, the force of gravity can be measured far more precisely.

6.1 Distinction between mass and force

To understand how gravity is used to measure force, we refer mainly to two laws: the Law of Universal Gravitation (section 4.8), and Newton's Second Law of Motion (section 4.7). The Law of Universal Gravitation states that the force of attraction between two bodies is proportional to the product of their masses and inversely proportional to the square of the distance between their centers. The force tending to draw the bodies together is of the same nature as the mechanical force which stretches a spring.

On the other hand, the mass of a body is the amount of matter which it contains, a quantity which stays constant regardless of where the body may be. In effect, the mass depends upon the number of atoms in the body and their nuclear composition. Mass and force are therefore entirely different physical quantities.

6.2 Using gravity to measure force

Suppose a body of known mass m is set on a platform. The body is pulled downwards by a force of gravity F, but the platform exerts an equal force upwards, with the result that the body remains stationary. How can we determine the magnitude of this downward force? A simple way is to let the body fall off the edge of the platform and measure the resulting acceleration g. Applying Newton's second law, we immediately obtain the result: $F = mg$.

The force of gravity calculated this way is the weight-force that the mass m exerts on the platform. If, at the same location, the known mass is replaced by another having a mass m', what is the new force of gravity? As before, we can measure the acceleration of free fall and calculate the resulting force F'. In so doing, we make the remarkable discovery, first observed by Galileo, that the acceleration of free fall, at a given location, is *absolutely constant*, irrespective of the mass of the body. Consequently, at a given location, a single measurement of g suffices to determine the weight-force exerted by any body of known mass.

6.3 Nature of the force of gravity

The force of gravity acting on a body is actually composed of several forces. The most important is the force *of gravitation* F_g exerted by the Earth. If the Earth were a perfect homogeneous sphere, the force would be given by

$$F_g = G \frac{m \, M}{d^2} \tag{6-1}$$

in which

F_g = force *of gravitation* acting on the body (not the force of gravity)
G = gravitational constant
m = mass of the body
M = mass of the Earth
d = distance of the body from the centre of the Earth

Unfortunately, the earth is an oblate spheroid having a complex inner structure and an equally complex surface, composed of mountains, valleys, oceans and plateaus. These individual masses all exert their gravitational forces on the given body, with the result that Eq 6-1 is only approximately true. Nevertheless, at a given location, the effective distance d and the effective mass M are constant, and consequently F_g is constant. On the other hand, if the body is moved to a new location, both the effective distance and the effective mass will be different. Thus, the force of gravitation varies with the location.

The spinning Earth also imparts a centripetal force to the body, whose magnitude depends likewise upon the location (see page 72). Finally, the moon and the sun exert additional, albeit minuscule, gravitational forces on the body. The sum of these forces constitutes what we conventionally call *the force of gravity*.

All these forces are themselves proportional to the mass m of the given body, and that is why the acceleration due to gravity, at a given location, is constant.

This important fact enables us to calculate the force of gravity at any selected location. For example, suppose we had to calculate the force of gravity exerted on a mass of 600 kg in Washington, D.C. The acceleration of a freely falling body at that location is known to be 9.800 83 m/s². Applying Newton's law $F = ma$, we find

$$F = 600 \text{ kg} \times 9.800 \, 83 \text{ m/ s}^2$$
$$= 5880.5 \text{ kg} \cdot \text{m/s}^2$$
$$= 5880.5 \text{ newtons}$$
$$= 5880.5 \text{ N}$$

If the same mass were transported to Paris, where the local acceleration of free fall is slightly higher (9.809 33 m/s²), the force pulling it down would be correspondingly greater:

$$F = ma$$
$$F = 600 \text{ kg} \times 9.809\ 33 \text{ m/ s}^2$$
$$= 5885.6 \text{ N}$$

6.4 Measuring the acceleration of free fall

The insert on pages 54 and 55 shows how the acceleration due to gravity was measured in the 1960s. It indicates the extreme care that had to be taken to attain an accuracy of one part in a million.

Today, some 30 years later, the acceleration of free fall is measured in a far more sophisticated way. Advances in technology enable accuracies of the order of one part in *one hundred* million, which represents an incredible improvement of two orders of magnitude. Such measurements are so accurate that they are even affected by the presence of newly-erected buildings in the vicinity of the testing laboratory.

6.5 Origin of kilogram-force and pound-force

The effective distance d from the center of the earth to any point on its surface is about 4000 miles and nowhere does this distance vary by more than a fraction of one percent. Because d is nearly constant, the force of gravity on a given mass varies only slightly as the mass is moved from place to place around the globe.

The constancy of the force of gravity can be appreciated even more by noting that when an object is raised 10 feet above the ground, the force acting on it decreases by only 1 part in a million. Suppose, for example, that the force of gravity acting on a mass of 1 kg located in Baltimore is 9.800 821 N. If the mass is raised 10 feet, the force of gravity will decrease by 0.000 0098 N, and the new force of gravity will be 9.800 811 N. For anything except very precise measurements, this is a negligible change.

Historically, the force of gravity on a mass of one kilogram was called the *kilogram-force*. However, it was known that the magnitude of the kilogram force varied slightly as the kilogram mass was moved from one place to another. The variation was evidenced by the slightly different acceleration of the body in free fall. In effect, the acceleration varies from a minimum of about 9.78 m/s² to a maximum of 9.83 m/s² over the face of the Earth.

In order to establish a definite, and scientifically undisputable value for the kilogram-force, it became necessary to choose and agree upon a standard of acceleration. The following list of accelerations, measured at several important laboratories, gives an idea of the range that was open to choice.

Laboratory	Location	Acceleration m/s²
Bureau international des poids et mesures	Sèvres, France	9.809 272
National Bureau of Standards	Washington, D.C.	9.800 821
National Research Council	Ottawa, Canada	9.806 132
All Union Institute of Metrology	Leningrad, USSR	9.819 187
National Physical Laboratory	Teddington, England	9.811 832

In 1901, at the Third General Conference of Weights and Measures, it was decided that the standard of acceleration would be 9.806 65 m/s² *exactly*. The kilogram-force was then defined as that force which will give a mass of one kilogram an acceleration of 9.806 65 m/s². Thus, from the equation $F = ma$

$$1 \text{ [kilogram-force]} = 9.806\ 65 \text{ [kg] [m/s}^2\text{]}$$

Consequently,

$$1 \text{ [kgf]} = 9.806\ 65 \left[\frac{\text{kg·m}}{\text{s}^2} \right] \tag{6-2}$$

Because the newton was later defined to be equal to 1 [kg·m/s²], it follows that one kilogram-force is exactly equal to 9.80665 N.

The pound-force was defined in a similar way. It is the force that will impart to a mass of one pound an acceleration of 9.80665 m/s². Thus,

$$1 \text{ [lbf]} = 1 \text{ [lb]} \times 9.806\ 65 \text{ [m/s}^2\text{]}$$

$$= \frac{453.592\ 37}{1000} \text{ [kg]} \times 9.806\ 65 \text{ [m/s}^2\text{]}$$

$$= 4.448\ 22 \frac{\text{kg·m}}{\text{s}^2}$$

$$= 4.448\ 22 \text{ N}$$

Note that in the English system, an acceleration of 9.806 65 m/s² corresponds exactly to 9.806 65 (×100) (÷12)(÷2.54) = 32.174 048 ··· [ft/s²].

In addition to the pound-force and the pound, the *poundal* and the *slug* are two other units that were defined in the English systems of units.

The poundal, a unit of force, is that force which will impart to a mass of 1 pound an acceleration of 1 foot per second per second.

The slug, a unit of mass, is that mass which will accelerate at a rate of 1 foot per second per second when subjected to a force of 1 pound-force.

6.6 Comments regarding mass and weight

We saw in equation (6-1) that the force of gravity acting on an object is directly proportional to its mass. When lifting or carrying an object, we are conscious of this force of gravity which continually tries to pull it downwards. As a result, we tend to think of the force as being the mass of the object. This subjective notion is incorrect because, as we know, a force is not the same thing as a mass.

Particular care must be taken when the term "pound" is used. The pound [lb], is a unit of mass. Depending on its location at the surface of the Earth, the force of gravity acting, say, on a 15 pound mass is very close to 15 pound-force [lbf]. Because the numerical values of force and mass are nearly the same, the name "pound-force" is often shortened to "pound", and this blurs the crucial distinction between force and mass.

To prevent confusion, the term *pound-force* (symbol lbf) should always be used when describing a force in the inch-pound-second system of units. Thus, a pressure that is loosely termed as "30 pounds per square inch" should really be stated as "30 pounds-force per square inch". Similarly, a torque of "5 foot pounds" should really be called "5 foot pound-force".

For the same reason, the kilogram-force (symbol kgf) should be used when describing force in non-SI metric systems. To get around the problem, some publications use the name *kilopond* instead of kilogram-force.

A further source of confusion is the meaning of the term "weight". It is usually associated with the force required to lift an object. Thus, from a strictly scientific viewpoint, weight means force of gravity. On the other hand, in the everyday world, weight is often considered to be a mass. For example, in measuring the weight of a bag of flour, we are interested in the mass of flour we are getting and not in the force of gravity that produces the reading on the scale.

The intended meaning of the words "weight" and "weigh" can usually be inferred from the context. The following examples show some of the ways these words are used and how they are interpreted.

STATEMENT	INTERPRETATION
"the weight of the car is 1200 kilograms	implies mass
"put one's weight on"	implies mass
"weight limit - 10 tons"	implies mass
"the roof collapsed under the weight of the snow"	implies force
"the weight of a body on the moon is only one sixth that on the Earth"	implies force

In technical work, a good rule is to avoid the terms "weight" and "weigh" whenever there is a possibility of confusing mass and force. Also to be avoided are incorrect statements such as "a force of 5 kilograms".

6.7 Comparison of masses

If two objects in close proximity and in vacuum are released at the same level above ground, they will accelerate at *exactly* the same rate. Under these conditions, the force of gravity acting on them depends exclusively upon their mass. This fact can be used to compare the masses of two objects with a beam balance.

A beam balance is in equilibrium when equal forces act on each side of the knife support, a property which makes this balance an excellent instrument to compare masses. Thus, if a standard 1 kilogram mass is precisely balanced in vacuum against any other object, we know that the forces are equal, and because the trays are at the same level, the masses must be the same.

Standards laboratories equipped with highly sophisticated balances can compare masses in this way with an accuracy of one part in one hundred million. It follows that the standard one kilogram mass kept in Sèvres, France, can be reproduced with high accuracy, thereby making this standard available throughout the world.

This transportable absolute gravimeter has a combined uncertainty of less than 1×10^{-7} m/s^2. (*Courtesy BIPM*)

7

DECIBELS AND NEPERS

In order to understand decibels and nepers, it is helpful to know the terminology and conventions that surround these units. In particular, we discuss the meaning of power ratio, field ratio, power level difference, field level difference and some of the reference standards that relate thereto.

7.1 Power ratio and amplitude ratio

The *power ratio* of a given power P and an arbitrary reference power P_0 is given by the expression

$$\text{power ratio} = P/P_0$$

where P_0, by definition, is in the denominator. P and P_0 are power quantities and they must be expressed in the same units so that their ratio yields a pure number. A power quantity is either power as such, or a quantity directly proportional to power, such as energy density, acoustic intensity or luminous intensity.

Some quantities, called *field* quantities, can be used as a proxy for power quantities. Voltage, current, sound pressure, velocity and electric field strength are typical field quantities. In electrotechnology, the field is usually a voltage or current, while in acoustics it is usually a pressure. In general, the square of a field quantity is proportional to power.

The *field ratio* of a given field F and an arbitrary reference field F_0 is given by

$$\text{field ratio} = F/F_0$$

where F_0, by definition, is in the denominator. The field quantities F and F_0 must be expressed in the same units so that their ratio is a pure number.

These ratios often cover a tremendous range, for example, 10^{-18} to 10^{+12}. For this and other reasons, it is convenient to use the *logarithm* of the ratios as a measure of the power ratio or the field ratio.

7.2 Power level difference

Power level difference (symbol L_P) is a physical quantity whose magnitude is related logarithmically to the power ratio, as follows:

$$\text{power level difference} = \log_{10}(\text{power ratio}) = \log(\text{power ratio})$$

which gives rise to the quantity equation:

$$L_P = \log\left(\frac{P}{P_o}\right)$$

The unit of power level difference is the **bel** (symbol B). One bel is the power level difference corresponding to a power ratio of 10. The **decibel** (symbol dB) is a submultiple of the bel, equal to 1/10 of a bel. In practice, the decibel is the preferred unit of power level difference.

The power level difference L_P is therefore given by the equation:

$$L_P = \{10 \log (P/P_o)\} \text{ [decibel]} \tag{7-1}$$

In this equation, the term in braces $\{10 \log (P/P_o)\}$ is the numerical value of the quantity, while [decibel] is the unit. As always, the logarithm is to the base 10.

For example, if the given power P is 12.6 W and the reference power P_o is 1 mW, the power level difference is

$$L_P = 10 \log (P/P_o) \text{ [dB]}$$
$$= 10 \log (12.6/0.001)$$
$$= 10 \log (12\ 600)$$
$$= 41 \text{ dB}$$

The magnitude of L_P may be positive, negative or zero, depending upon whether P is greater than, less than, or equal to the reference P_o.

In some publications, the unit of power level difference is the *neper* (symbol Np). By *definition*, the magnitude of the power level difference is then expressed by

$$L_P = \{0.5 \ln (P/P_o)\} \text{ [neper]} \tag{7-2}$$

Note that in this case, the numerical value $\{0.5 \ln (P/P_o)\}$ is expressed in terms of the natural logarithm of the power ratio.

From equations (7-1) and (7-2) we can readily deduce that the [neper] is larger than the [decibel], the relationship being

$$1 \text{ [Np]} = 20/(\ln 10) \text{ [dB]}$$

thus, $1 \text{ [Np]} = 8.685\ 890 \text{ [dB]}$

Referring to the previous example, a power level difference of 41 dB is the same as a power level difference of 41 ($\div$ 8.685 890) Np = 4.72 Np.

7.3 Field level difference

Field level difference (symbol L_F) is a physical quantity whose magnitude is related logarithmically to the field ratio. The unit of field level difference is also the decibel. However, *by definition*, the magnitude of L_F is given by

$$L_F = \{20 \log (F/F_o)\} \text{ [decibels]} \tag{7-3}$$

Note that the coefficient preceding the logarithm in equation (7-3), is different from that in equation (7-1) because the factor 10 is replaced by the factor 20.

For example, if the reference voltage E_0 across a load is 3 V while the actual voltage E is 72 mV, the field level difference L_F is

$$L_F = 20 \log (E/E_0) \, [\text{dB}]$$

$$= 20 \log 0.072 / 3$$

$$= -32.4 \, \text{dB}$$

The decibel value is negative because the actual voltage E is less than the reference voltage.

Whenever the nature of the field is known (voltage, current, pressure, etc.) the field level difference L_F is expressed in terms of voltage, current, pressure, etc. Thus, in the above example, L_F is called the *voltage* level difference. Similarly, in acoustics, we speak of a *pressure* level difference.

The neper is also used as a unit of field level difference. In this case, by *definition*, the field level difference L_F is given by the expression

$$L_F = \ln (F/F_0) \, [\text{neper}]$$

The relationship between the neper and the decibel remains the same as before:

$$1 \, [\text{Np}] = 8.685 \; 890 \, [\text{dB}]$$

$$\text{or} \quad 1 \, [\text{B}] = 1.151 \; 29 \, [\text{Np}]$$

7.4 Relationship between L_P and L_F

In comparing equations (7-1) and (7-3) one may ask why different factors (10 and 20) were chosen for L_P and L_F. The reason is that in many practical cases, the square of the amplitude of a voltage, current or pressure can be used as a proxy for the power at the point of measurement.

For example, in electrotechnology, for a fixed impedance, the power is proportional to the square of the voltage E. This enables us to express the power level difference L_P in terms of the voltage level difference $L_{F(\text{voltage})}$, as follows:

$$L_P = 10 \log (P/P_0)$$

$$= 10 \log (E/E_0)^2$$

$$= 20 \log (E/E_0)$$

$$= L_{F \, (\text{voltage})}$$

Thus, when the impedance is fixed, $L_P = L_{F \,(\text{voltage})}$. In other words, the field level difference L_F yields the same decibel value as we would obtain if we measured the power level difference L_P directly, such as with a wattmeter.

It is usually much easier to measure a voltage, current or pressure than the actual power, and so the concept of field level difference L_F is useful in the determination of L_P.

Example 7-1:

The input power at the antenna of a radio is $1\mu W$ and the power output at the speaker is 40 mW. What is the power gain in decibels ?

Solution:

The power ratio is $40\,mW/1\mu W = 40\,000$. The power gain (power level difference) is therefore:

$$\text{Power level difference } L_P = 10 \log 40\,000$$

$$= 46 \text{ dB}$$

Example 7-2:

After surrounding a machine with acoustic insulation, the sound pressure decreased from 16 Pa to 0.24 Pa. What is the decrease in pressure, expressed in dB ?

Solution:

Using the initial pressure as a reference, the field ratio is $0.24/16 = 0.015$, which corresponds to a field level difference of $L_F = 20 \log 0.015 = -36.5$ dB. Since there is a pressure decrease, the decibel value is negative.

In some unusual cases, the power level may not be proportional to the square of the field quantity. For example, the acoustic intensity produced by a fan varies approximately as the *fifth* power of the speed of rotation. Consequently, if the speed N is used as a proxy for acoustic intensity (which itself is proportional to power) the power level difference is given by

$$L_P = 10 \log \frac{P_N}{P_{N0}} \text{ [dB]}$$

in which

P_N = acoustic intensity at actual speed, in r/min

P_{N0} = acoustic intensity at reference speed, in r/min

On the other hand, if the field ratio N/N_0 is used as a proxy for acoustic intensity, we would obtain the following expression for the field level difference:

$$L_{F\,(r/min)} = 10 \log \left(\frac{N}{N_0}\right)^5$$

thus $\qquad L_{F\,(r/min)} = 50 \log \frac{N}{N_0} \text{ [dB]}$

Note that in this special case the factor 50 replaces the usual factor 20.

7.5 Standardized field levels and power levels

In science and engineering, it has been found convenient to establish a few standardized amplitudes and powers in order to use them as reference levels. For example, the international standard for the sound power radiated by a source has been standardized at 1 picowatt. Thus, $P_o = P$ (ref 1 picowatt) $= 10^{-12}$ W.

Similarly, the field reference for sound pressure has been standardized at 20 micropascals. These standards enable us to express a given acoustic power as an *absolute* sound power level. Similarly, a given pressure level can be expressed as an absolute pressure level.

In electrical work, the standardized reference power is 1 mW. Consequently, a power of 10 kW corresponds to an absolute power level of

$$L_P = 10 \log P/P_{(\text{ref } 1 \text{ mW})}$$

$$= 10 \log (10^4/10^{-3})$$

thus $\quad L_P$ (ref 1 mW) $= 70$ dB

When absolute power or pressure levels are given, it is important to state the reference power or pressure that was used in making the calculation.

Example 7-3:

Calculate the absolute sound pressure level for a sound having an acoustic pressure of 1.2 Pa.

Solution:

$$L_F = 20 \log P/P_{(\text{ref } 20 \mu\text{Pa})}$$

$$= 20 \log \frac{1.2}{20 \times 10^{-6}}$$

$$= 95.56 \text{ dB}$$

hence $\quad L_F$ (ref 20 μPa) $= 95.56$ dB

7.6 The decibel as a measure of other quantities

Although the decibel is related to the ratio of two powers, it is sometimes extended to include the ratio of other quantities, even when power, as such, is not directly involved. For example, in the measurement of the sensitivity of microphones, an open-circuit voltage of 1 volt produced by a sound pressure level of 1 pascal is defined as being a sensitivity of zero dB.

Instruments which measure sound and noise are also calibrated in decibels (ref 20 μPa). However, they are generally weighted in a special way to reflect the subjective response of the human ear to different frequencies. The International Electrotechnical Commission (of which the United States, Canada and most countries of the world are members) recognizes three types of frequency response curves, designated as A, B and C. The reading in dB of a sound level meter must specify the response curve that was used. As a matter of interest, a sound level of 20 dB(A) is just audible, 70 dB(A) corresponds to normal conversation, and a sound level of 120 dB(A) is on the threshold of pain.*

Example 7-4:

A 10-watt loudspeaker produces a sound intensity of 80 dB(A). If it is replaced by four such speakers, what total sound intensity will they produce?

Solution:

The four loudspeakers will not produce 320 dB(A), as we might be inclined to believe. We must add the powers of the four speakers, which amounts to 40 watts. Since the original power was 10 W and the new power is 40 W (a power ratio of 4), the power level difference is:

$$L_P = 10 \log \frac{P}{P_0} = 10 \log (40/10) = 6 \text{ dB}$$

Consequently, the four loudspeakers produce an output of $(80 + 6) = 86$ dB(A).

7.7 Deriving power ratios and field ratios from dB values

We can readily calculate the power ratios and field ratios when the power level difference or field level difference is given. Thus, it can be shown that

$$\text{field ratio} = \frac{F}{F_0} = 10^{L_F/20} \qquad (7\text{-}4)$$

$$\text{power ratio} = \frac{P}{P_0} = 10^{L_P/10} \qquad (7\text{-}5)$$

Example 7-5:

A manufacturer's brochure states that a particular condenser microphone has a sensitivity of -60 dB (ref 1V/μbar). Express these specifications in terms that do not involve decibels.

Solution:

Since the sensitivity is -60 dB, the microphone output is 60 dB below 1 volt when the pressure is 1 μbar. This corresponds to a field (voltage) ratio of:

$$\text{field ratio} = \frac{F}{F_0} = 10^{L_F/20} \qquad (7\text{-}4)$$

$$\frac{F}{F_0} = 10^{-60/20} = 10^{-3} = 1/1000$$

The sensitivity of the microphone is therefore $1/1000 \times 1$V/μbar, or 1mV/μbar, which is equivalent to 10 mV/Pa.

---

* Note that the symbol (A) merely indicates how the sound level was determined; it does not change the meaning or the magnitude of the decibel unit.

8

DERIVING UNITS FROM BASE UNITS

As we have seen, all measurement systems involve quantities and units. These systems are built upon a few base quantities (mass, length, time, etc.) and a corresponding number of base units (kilogram, meter, second, etc.).

8.1 Dimension of quantities

In the SI, all quantities can be expressed in terms of seven base quantities. Restricting ourselves to the base quantities mass, length and time (M, L, T), we can derive quantities such as area, volume, acceleration and force.

When a derived quantity is expressed in terms of base quantities, we call this the "dimension" of the quantity. Thus the dimension of area is L^2, that of acceleration is LT^{-2}, that of density is ML^{-3}, while that of force is MLT^{-2}. If, in addition, we add the base quantity for electric current (I), we can show that the dimension of a derived quantity such as magnetic flux is $ML^2T^{-2}I^{-1}$.

Some derived quantities, such as the plane angle and the solid angle are "dimensionless" because they are respectively the ratio of two lengths and the ratio of two areas. In reality, their dimension is unity, i.e. the simple number 1.

Dimensions are useful in checking the validity and the "balance" of physical equations, in the sense that the dimensions on the left-hand side must balance those on the right-hand side. This is no trivial matter, as is evidenced in James Clerk Maxwell's book *A Treatise on Electricity and Magnetism*, first published in 1873. In effect, by analyzing the dimension of the quantities used respectively in the electrostatic (esu) and electromagnetic (emu) systems of measurement, he discovered that the two systems were related by a quantity having the dimension of velocity. This velocity turned out to be the speed of light, which laid the groundwork for Maxwell's famous equations on the propagation of electromagnetic waves.

8.2 Derived units in terms of base units

By analogy with the dimension of a derived quantity in terms of base quantities, it is possible to express a derived unit in terms of base units. In effect, all derived units of the SI stem from the base units (meter, kilogram, second, ampere, kelvin, mole and candela); consequently, the units of power, voltage, magnetic flux, and so forth, can be expressed in terms of m, kg, s, A, K, mol and cd. Thus, the SI unit of area is m^2, of acceleration is m/s^2, of density is kg/m^3, and of force is $kg \cdot m/s^2$.

The expression in base units of the units of force, power, voltage, magnetic flux, etc., are displayed in brackets at the left-hand side of each conversion chart.

Some derived units in the SI can be expressed advantageously in other than base units. For example, the pascal, a unit of pressure, may be expressed as N/m^2 or as $kg/(m{\cdot}s^2)$. The expression $kg/(m{\cdot}s^2)$ is in terms of base units, while N/m^2 is the expression in terms of a derived unit having a special name (N) and a base unit (m).

8.3 Expressing a derived unit in terms of base units

To express a derived unit in terms of base units, we must know two things:

1. The definition of the derived unit,
2. The quantity equation which relates the derived unit to units whose expressions in terms of base units are known.

For example, let us express the [newton] in terms of base units. The SI definition states that "the newton is that force which gives to a mass of one kilogram an acceleration of one meter per second per second". The quantity equation is

$$F = ma$$

Based upon the SI definition, we can write:

one [newton] = one [kilogram] × one [meter per second per second]

$$1 \text{ [N]} = 1 \text{ [kg]} \times 1 \text{ [m/s}^2\text{]}$$

whence $N = kg{\cdot}m{\cdot}s^{-2}$

Knowing the expression for the newton, we can now determine a similar expression for the joule. By definition, "the joule is the work done when the point of application of one newton is displaced a distance of one meter in the direction of the force".

The quantity equation is
$$E = Fd$$
that is, work = force × distance

Using the SI definition and the quantity equation, we can write:

one [joule] = one [newton] × one [meter]

$$1 \text{ [J]} = 1 \text{ [N]} \times 1 \text{ [m]}$$

thus $J = N{\cdot}m$

but since $N = kg{\cdot}m{\cdot}s^{-2}$

we obtain $J = kg{\cdot}m^2{\cdot}s^{-2}$

and so the expression for the joule in terms of base units is $kg{\cdot}m^2{\cdot}s^{-2}$.

We are now in position to express the [watt] in terms of base units. By definition, "the watt is the power which gives rise to the production of energy at the rate of one joule per second". The quantity equation is

$$P = E/t$$

$$\text{that is,} \quad \text{power} = \frac{\text{energy}}{\text{time}}$$

Using the SI definition, we can therefore write:

$$\text{one [watt]} = \frac{\text{one [joule]}}{\text{one [second]}}$$

$$1 \text{ [W]} = \frac{1 \text{ [J]}}{1 \text{ [s]}}$$

$$\text{therefore} \quad W = J \cdot s^{-1}$$

$$\text{but since} \quad J = kg \cdot m^2 \cdot s^{-2}$$

$$\text{we obtain} \quad W = kg \cdot m^2 \cdot s^{-3}$$

and so the expression for the watt in terms of base units is $kg \cdot m^2 \cdot s^{-3}$.

Let us now express the [volt] in terms of base units. By definition, "one volt is the difference of potential between two points of a conducting wire carrying a constant current of one ampere, when the power dissipated between these points is equal to one watt".

The quantity equation is

$$E = P/I$$

that is,

$$\text{electromotive force} = \frac{\text{power}}{\text{current}}$$

Using the SI definition of the volt in the quantity equation, we can write:

$$\text{one [volt]} = \frac{\text{one [watt]}}{\text{one [ampere]}}$$

$$1 \text{ [V]} = \frac{1 \text{ [W]}}{1 \text{ [A]}}$$

$$\text{therefore} \quad V = W \cdot A^{-1}$$

but since $W = kg \cdot m^2 \cdot s^{-3}$

we obtain $V = kg \cdot m^2 \cdot A^{-1} \cdot s^{-3}$

and so the expression for the volt in terms of base units is $kg \cdot m^2 \cdot A^{-1} \cdot s^{-3}$.

Consider now the unit of magnetic flux. By definition, "the **weber** (Wb) is the magnetic flux which, linking a circuit of one turn, produces in it an electromotive force of 1 volt as it is reduced to zero at a uniform rate in one second".

The relevant quantity equation is based on Faraday's Law of Electromagnetic Induction, namely

$$E = N \frac{d\phi}{dt}$$

which means

electromotive force = *number* of turns × rate of change of magnetic flux.

Appying the definition of the weber in this equation, we have

one [volt] = 1 × one [weber] per [one second]

hence $[V] = \dfrac{[Wb]}{[s]}$

Therefore Wb = V·s, but since $V = kg \cdot m^2 \cdot A^{-1} \cdot s^{-3}$, we obtain

$$Wb = kg \cdot m^2 \cdot A^{-1} \cdot s^{-2}$$

Thus, the expression for the weber in terms of base units is $kg \cdot m^2 \cdot A^{-1} \cdot s^{-2}$.

The expressions of derived units in terms of base units are found, therefore, by a pyramiding process in which each successive derived unit becomes the stepping-stone to establish the next. That is how the expression of each derived unit (displayed between brackets [ ] in the charts) was established. However, it is important to remember that these expressions are derived from the definitions of the SI system of measurement.

Older metric systems defined the units in a different way, and so the resulting expressions were quite different from those of the SI. For example, the statcoulomb, based upon the centimeter-gram-second (esu) system, had the expression $[cm^{1.5} g^{0.5} s^{-1}]$.

As mentioned earlier, the expression for a derived unit can often be expressed in different ways, some of which have a definite physical meaning. Consider for example, some of the expressions that can be given to the [volt]:

$$[volt] = \frac{[watt]}{[ampere]} \qquad (1)$$

$$= \frac{[joule]}{[ampere] \, [\,second]} \qquad (2)$$

$$= \frac{[joule]}{[coulomb]} \qquad (3)$$

$$= \frac{[newton\text{-}meter]}{[coulomb]} \qquad (4)$$

$$= [ampere] \, [ohm] \qquad (5)$$

$$= \frac{[kilogram] \, [meter]^2}{[ampere][second]^3} \qquad (6)$$

Some of these expressions defy physical interpretation, but expression (1) corresponds to the SI definition of the volt, while expression (3) corresponds to its physical definition: one volt is the difference of potential between two points when one joule of work is done in transporting one coulomb of charge. Expression (5) is a reflection of Ohm's law.

MEASUREMENTS AND INTERNATIONAL STANDARDS

Measurements impinge, to an increasingly important extent, on the industrial, scientific, commercial, and legal affairs of the world. In virtually all the industrialized nations it is now recognized that there must be, on a national basis, a clear structure within which these various and largely complementary aspects of metrology can be placed. In many countries a national measurement network is already in place and in others one is being established. The need for nations to have a mutually acceptable structure within which reliable measurements can be made and verified has recently taken on a new importance. Such mutual acceptance requires assured uniformity of measurement.

The intergovernmental agreement under which uniformity of measurement is assured is the Convention du Mètre, signed in Paris in 1875, and resulting in the establishment of the Bureau international des poids et mesures (BIPM) at Sèvres. Nearly fifty nations adhere to the Convention, among which are all of the major industrialized nations.

International trade in high technology products, communication and navigation networks, the exchange of scientific information, as well as a multitude of pure and applied scientific and technological projects carried out on an international basis, are all highly dependent upon precise measurement. Indeed, the actual process of the manufacture of any product is totally dependent upon traceability of measurements to national and thence to international measurement standards.

Within each country the national laboratory is at the focus of the national measurement network and is the link with other national laboratories and the BIPM. The national laboratories and the BIPM working together provide the key to the world-wide uniformity and the coordinated progress in measurement, which together constitute one of the foundations of the industrialized world.

The BIPM is situated on the outskirts of Paris. The principal building shown here is the Pavillon de Breteuil. Other surrounding buildings house various standards laboratories. (*Courtesy BIPM*)

The Convention du Mètre, as well as founding the BIPM, established a permanent organizational structure of member goverments to act in common accord on all matters relating to units of measurement.

Under the terms of the Convention, The BIPM operates under the exclusive supervision of the Comité international de poids et mesures (CIPM) which itself comes under the authority of the Conférence générale des poids et mesures (CGPM). The CGPM elects the members of CIPM and brings together, periodically, the representatives of the governments of member nations.

Among its duties, the CGPM discusses and examines the arrangements required to ensure the propagation and improvement of the International System of Units (SI); it

Note: This box is a highly abridged version of the text material found in the BIPM publication "Le BIPM et la Convention du Mètre". Permission obtained, courtesy of BIPM.

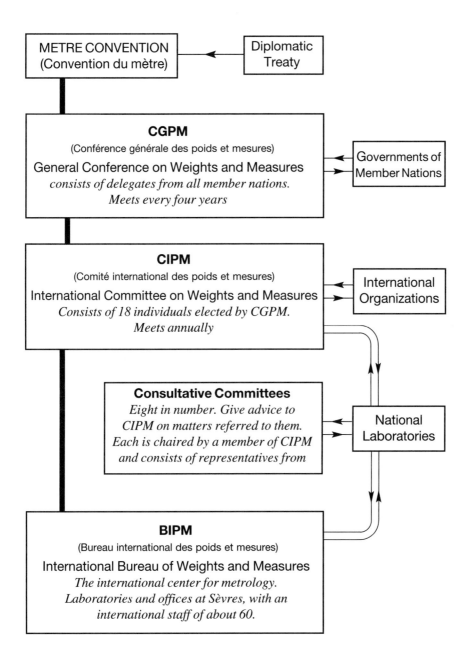

International structure of standards-setting bodies.

endorses the results of new fundamental metrological determinations; and it adopts the important decisions concerning the organization and development of the BIPM.

The CIPM oversees and directs the work of the BIPM. It issues an Annual Report on the administrative and financial position of the BIPM to the Governments of the Member States of the Convention du Mètre. The CIPM has created a set of Consultative Committees bringing together the world's experts in the specified fields as advisers on scientific and technical matters. There are eight committees whose expertise cover such fields as electricity, photometry, thermometry, length, time, mass, ionizing radiation and units of measurement.

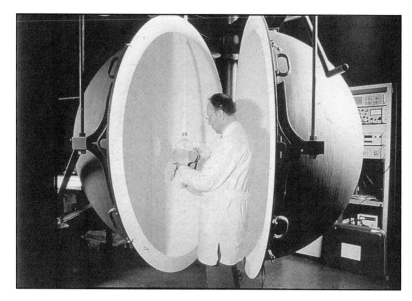

This 1.5 m integrating sphere is used to measure the total light output of luminous sources. It enables a precise measurement of the amount of luminous flux, in lumens. (*Courtesy BIPM*)

The CIPM and BIPM also work in close cooperation with other intergovernmental and international organizations concerned with metrology. For example, there are close links with the International Organization for Legal Metrology, the International Electrotechnical Commission, the International Commission on Illumination, the International Union on Radio Science, the International Union of Pure and Applied Physics, and ISO.

This brief account shows that the world's measurement network involves a complex web of official and unofficial agreements and working relationships. The Convention du Mètre through the CGPM, the CIPM and the BIPM, provides the formal and physical basis for measurement upon which all other international activity in practical metrology is founded.

BIBLIOGRAPHY

Ambler, E., 1971. *SI Units, Philosophical Basis for the Base Units*. Technical News Bulletin, March 1971. Washington, DC. National Bureau of Standards.

ANSI/IEEE, 1992. *American National Standard for Metric Practice*. (ANSI/IEEE Std 268-1992). New York. Institute of Electrical and Electronics Engineers.

ASME, 1975-1982. *ASME SI SERIES SI-1 TO SI-10*: New York. The American Society of Mechanical Engineers.

ASTM, 1991. *Standard Practice for Use of the SI International System of Units (ASTM E380-91a)*. Philadelphia, PA. American Society for Testing and Materials.

____, 1987. *Standard Practice for Conversion of Kinematic Viscosity to Saybolt Universal Viscosity or to Saybolt Fural Viscosity*. Philadelphia, PA. American Society for Testing and Materials.

BIPM, 1991. *Le système international d'unités* (SI) 6e édition, textes français et anglais. Sèvres, France. Bureau international des poids et mesures.

____, 1987. *Le BIPM et la convention du mètre*. Sèvres, France. Bureau international des poids et mesures. [This English/French document describes measurement techniques used in establishing SI standards.]

____, 1990. *Techniques for Approximating the International Temperature Scale of 1990*. Sèvres, France. Bureau international des poids et mesures.

____, 1990. *Supplementary Information for the International Temperature Scale of 1990*. Sèvres, France. Bureau international des poids et mesures.

Cohen, E.R. and Giacomo, P. 1987. International Union of Pure and Applied Physics. *Symbols, Units, Nomenclature and Fundamental Constants in Physics*. Document I.U.P.A.P.-25. Netherlands.

Cohen, E.R. and Taylor B.N. 1986. *The 1986 Adjustment of the Fundamental Physical Constants*. Codata Bulletin. New York. Pergamon.

CSA, 1989. *Canadian Metric Practice Guide. CAN/CSA-Z 234.1-89*. Toronto. Canadian Standards Association.

Drazil, J.V. 1983. *Quantities and Units of Measurement*. London. Mansell Publishing.

Engrand, J.C. 1981. *Units and Their Equivalences*. Paris. Vuibert.

Horvath, A.L. 1987. *Conversion Tables of Units for Science and Engineering*. New York. Elsevier.

ICRU, 1980. *Radiation Quantities and Units*, ICRU Report 33. Washington, DC. International Commission of Radiation Quantities and Units.

IEC, 1989. *Logarithmic Quantities and Units, IEC – Publication 27-3.* 3, rue de Varembé, Geneva 20, Switzerland, CH-1211. International Electrotechnical Commission.

_____, 1972. *Letter Symbols to Be Used in Electrical Technology, IEC – Publication 27-2.* Geneva. International Electrotechnical Commission.

ISO, 1992. ISO – 31 *Series.* 1, rue de Varembé, Geneva 20, Switzerland, CH-1211. International Organization for Standardization.

_____, 1984 *International Vocabulary of Basic and General Terms in Metrology*

IUPAC, 1993. *Quantities, Units and Symbols in Physical Chemistry.* Oxford, U.K. Blackwood Scientific Publications Ltd.

Ipsen, D.C. 1960. *Units, Dimensions and Dimensionless Numbers.* New York. M^{C}Graw-Hill.

Judson, L.V. 1976. *Weights and Measures Standards of the United States: A Brief History* (publication 247). Washington, DC. Superintendent of Documents, U.S. Government Printing Office.

Martinek, A. 1977. *Metric System (SI) in Engineering Technology.* Waterloo. Reeve Bean.

Maxwell, J.C. 1954. *A Treatise on Electricity and Magnetism,* Vol. 2 Chaps X and XI. New York. Dover Publications.

M&C and ME, 1990. *Home Study Course.* Pittsburgh, PA. Measurements & Control Magazine, Medical Electronics Magazine.

NIST, 1991. *The International System of Units (SI), Special Publication 330.* Washington, DC. National Institute of Standards and Technology.

Preston-Thomas, H. et al. 1968. *An Absolute Measurement of the Acceleration Due to Gravity.* NRC Publication 5693. Ottawa. National Research Council of Canada.

USMA, 1992. *Freeman Training/Education Metric Materials List.* Northridge, CA. U.S. Metric Association.

Wildi, T. 1970. *Units. Québec.* Volta.

_____, 1972. *Understanding Units.* Québec. Volta.

_____, 1988. *Units and Conversion Charts.* Québec. Sperika Enterprises Ltd.

_____, 1991. *Units and Conversion Charts – The Metrification Handbook for Engineers and Scientists.* Piscataway, NJ. IEEE Press.

Young, L. 1969. *Systems of Units in Electricity and Magnetism.* Edinburgh. Oliver and Boyd.

Zupko, R.E. 1968. *A Dictionary of English Weights and Measures.* Madison, WI. University of Wisconsin Press.

ANSWERS TO REVIEW QUESTIONS

CHAPTER 1

1) 2.04 atm   2) 5121.6 Btu/h   3) 200 Btu/min   4) 0.279 lb.ft^2 5) 15.551 728 kg

6) *m, E, P*   7) kg, V/m, W   8) kg.m^{-1}.s^{-2}, kg.m^{-1}.s^{-1}, m.s^{-1} 9a) 22.22 °C   9b) 40 °C

10) 1.183 L   11) 17.003 62   12) 17 463   13) 987 654 321.123 456 78

14) 1700.364 29

CHAPTER 2

5) newton (N), pascal (Pa), joule (J), radian (rad), watt (W), hertz (Hz)

6) hecto, kilo, mega, deci, centi, milli, micro, nano 7) mL   8) TJ   9) MPa   10) kHz

11) MΩ   12) cm   13) mg   14) kmol   15) mW   16) mrad   17) kN   18) mT   19) ns

20) pF   21) pA   22) kV   23) km   24) μWb

CHAPTER 3

1) 3.2808   2) 0.025 400   3) 1054.4   4) 2.2046   5) 0.224 81   6) 3.7854

7) 0.239 01   8) 0.023 565   9) 0.009 8692   10) 1.311 in^2 11) 2.59 km^2

12) 98.095 kW   13) 23.9 cal/s 14) 1.627 kW   15) 3 mA/m^2 16) 0.432 GJ

17) 106.76 N   18) 96.522 pdl   19) 1.4175 kg   20) 13.166 oz (avdp)

21) 205.57 slugs   22) 2.6998 nautical miles   23) 2152.8 lx   24) 2×10^{-7} T

25) 76.861 fl oz (U.S.)   26) 1.938 kg·m^2 27) 9.332 mm Hg(0 °C)   28) 1.2×10^6 Mx

29) 0.1992 μrad/s   30) 238.73 r/min   31) 24 μT

CHAPTER 4

1) 619.35 cm^2 2) 66 890 cm^3 3) 453.07 kg   4) 22.81 N.s   5) 30.48 J   6) 523.6 W

7) 907.19 mol   8) 3.968 Btu   9) 25.53 m/s   10) 0.671 mi   11) 198.19 kg

12) 2061.3 kg   13) 320.17 r/min   14) 29.88 m/s   15) 8.4742 N·m   16) 3.08 hp

17) 61.62 ft/s   18) 1.6344 m/s^2 19) 639.92 J   20) 29.67 h   21) 11 523 J, 11 523 N

22) 0.8884 MJ   23) 6090Yg   24a) 841.04 K   24b) 567.89 °C

25) 67.386 kPa

CHAPTER 5

1) **F = MA**   2) **F = MA**   3) **P** $= 1.904 \times 10^{-4}$ **WT**   4) **F** $=1.062 \times 10^{-6}$ **BLI**

5) **F** $= 3.4084 \times 10^{-4}$ **MW^{2}R**   6) **B = H**   7) **PV** $= 0.023 659$ **n** (**T$_F$** $+ 459.67$)

8) $A = wl$ 9) $v = \omega r$ 10) $F = 8.9875 \times 10^9$ (kg.m^3.A^{-2}. s^{-3}) $q_1 q_2/d^2$

11) $F = 398\,585$ (m.H^{-1}) $B^2 A$ 12) $W = 0.06579$ s.K$^{-0.5}$.m^{-1} $d^2 (IP/T)^{0.5}$

note: H = henry, T = thermodynamic temperature

INDEX

FOR REFERENCE

Do Not Take From This Room